Praise for
The Undertaker's Wife

The Undertaker's Wife confirms the fact that real life is stranger than fiction. Filled with poignant, honest, and lots of hilarious moments, this is a fun read, with plenty of food for thought. You'll be glad you chose this one. Enjoy!

TERRY MEEUWSEN, cohost, *The 700 Club*

Fast-paced with richly developed characters, *The Undertaker's Wife* is a witty and poignant story of faith and family. Dee Oliver tells her story with a tender humor that provides a powerful message to all of us as we confront the unexpected challenges life—and death—provide. An enjoyable and moving read.

BRIGADIER GENERAL ANTHONY J. TATA (U.S. Army, retired), bestselling author of *Foreign and Domestic*

The Undertaker's Wife is a beautifully written memoir about love and loss, and about learning to trust God through it all. Dee's story is both tender and funny, and ultimately a poignant reminder about the powerful gift of prayer.

JEANNIE CUNNION, author of *Parenting the Wholehearted Child*

In the world of running, how you train can make all the difference—and it's the same thing on the track of life. Many thanks to Dee Oliver for writing about grief and loss in a way that will help all of us prepare to finish the race with strength, dignity, and even a little laughter along the way.

THE HONORABLE JIM RYUN, five-term Congre~ ~an, three-ti~   ~n

Where humor meets God and takes the stin~ regardless of our race, economic status to the funeral!

SUSAN ALEXANDER Ya   ~or.

In *The Undertaker's Wife*, Dee Oliver has opened a coffin for us and found a laughing body. She has scripted out a poignant, hilarious, and practical autobiographical work that laughs at a death that may yet make us weep, but has lost its sting. Here is a lived theology of Resurrection in the midst of traveling through a valley of tears. Like Chaucer's Wife of Bath, Dee may have sent her husband on to Jesus, but by the end of the book, we want to travel the rest of our journey heavenward with her. We know it will be an inspired hoot of a story, just like this marvelous book.

TERRY LINDVALL, C. S. Lewis Chair of Communication and Christian Thought, Virginia Wesleyan College

I laughed, I cried, I took notes! *The Undertaker's Wife* is a hilarious, uniquely Southern rendering of mourning, empathy, fortitude, and loving others well in times of need.

SUSAN MERRILL, director of content at Family First, iMOM.com, AllProDad.com, FamilyMinute.com

Plenty of funeral directors can speak with wisdom and authority, but Dee is that rare breed of professional who can also do it with wit and grace. Don't be fooled by the entertainment value of this memoir. You might laugh—or cry—but in the end, you'll have read a very important work about life, death, and how to bridge the gaps that both can leave.

WILL SESSOMS, mayor of Virginia Beach

Southern women have found their Mark Twain in Dee Oliver! Traversing the tale of her life from single woman to widowed mother of three, Dee connects the dots between love and loss and limns a winsome picture of how God's grace turns stumbling blocks into stepping stones, and despair into hope for the future.

THE REVEREND ANDREW BUCHANAN, rector of Galilee Church

The Undertaker's Wife

A Memoir

A TRUE STORY of LOVE, LOSS, and LAUGHTER IN THE UNLIKELIEST of PLACES

DEE OLIVER

WITH JODIE BERNDT

ZONDERVAN®

ZONDERVAN

The Undertaker's Wife
Copyright © 2015 by Dee Branch Oliver and Jodie Berndt

This title is also available as a Zondervan ebook. Visit www.zondervan.com/ebooks.

Requests for information should be addressed to:

Zondervan, 3900 *Sparks Dr. SE, Grand Rapids, Michigan* 49546

ISBN 978-0-310-34083-6

Cover design: James Hall
Cover photography: UnoPix / iStockphoto® / Wikimedia Commons
Interior design: Katherine Lloyd, The DESK

First Printing January 2015 / Printed in the United States of America

To Johnnie . . .

Contents

IT. HAS. BEEN.
A. YEAR!

I lay awake in bed, staring at the ceiling. The two dogs were asleep near my feet, having staked their territory on my Yves Delorme duvet months ago. Down the hall, my three daughters slept peacefully in their rooms.

May 2, 2008. People say the first year is the hardest — the first Christmas, the first Father's Day, the first wedding anniversary without your spouse — but I couldn't imagine life getting any easier. I'd made it through the first twelve months; only God knew how many more months — or years — I had to go. What if I never got remarried? Could I really live like this, with dogs in my bed instead of a man, for the rest of my life?

I looked down at the dogs. They needed a bath. Johnnie would have kicked them off. He liked things neat and tidy, organized, and efficient. Dogs on the bed were not part of his plan.

But then, neither was dying.

The house was so quiet that time of morning. I slipped out of the sheets, reaching for my robe and pulling back my long brown hair into a ponytail. I'd had it colored last week; that, at least, was something I could control. If nothing else went right on the anniversary of Johnnie's death, at least my hair would look good.

Ever faithful, the dogs followed me downstairs, their paws making only the softest clicks on the hardwood floor of our kitchen. I let them out and started the coffee. As it brewed, my mind retraced the milestones of my adult life. I had checked a lot of boxes.

Travel through Europe? Check.

Go to college? Check, perhaps double checked. I'd had a lot of fun!

Live on my own with a bunch of girlfriends, holding down jobs that didn't get in the way of our social lives? Check.

Find a handsome and wealthy doctor to marry?

Not checked.

All of my life I'd had an irrational and yet ever-present fear of getting sick, so sick that I might die. If I married a doctor, I reasoned, I could take ill at any moment, even during the middle of the night, and I would have instant access to first-class medical care. The fact that he would be a *handsome* doctor was a given. Like UPS men, the doctors I'd known seemed, both on television and in person, to be square-jawed, physically fit, and generally attractive men. And the stipulation that my doctor-husband would, of necessity, be *wealthy* was something I'd picked up from my mother, a woman who taught me how to drink (one glass of wine at a party; the bottle at home, if needed), how to make the most of a hospital stay (if you have to have, say, a hysterectomy, you "might as well call the plastic surgeon for a little nip too, darling"), and how to hold it together in the face of pain, sorrow, and unruly children (a neat trick that usually involved a new dress and, almost as often, a flight to Paris). As Mother routinely opined when dishing up nuptial advice, "You can fall in love with a rich man as easily as you can a poor one."

Well, I never found the doctor. Instead, I fell in love with Johnnie, whose occupation I had, at the starry-eyed age of twenty-one, never even heard of. He was a funeral director. Which, when I stopped to think about it, was even better. Funeral directors couldn't die; they had to stick around so they could bury everyone else, right? And surely this Teflon-coated protection would cover both him and me, his loving and supportive spouse.

So much for logic.

After pouring myself a large mug of coffee, I grabbed my Bible and headed outside to sit on the front steps, where the hydrangeas Johnnie had planted (well, the ones he had paid somebody to plant) were just beginning to bloom. I had never prayed all that much before Johnnie died, but with no one else to confide in, I didn't mind when God stepped into the gap. I never felt like he was judging me for waiting so long to talk to him; instead, it seemed as if he had all the time in the world (which I guess he did — or does) and he was just glad I was there. Anyway, I hadn't missed a day with God during the past year. With bills to pay, rotten windows to replace, and three daughters to raise, I needed all the help I could get, and talking things over with God in the morning had become as much a part of my widowed life as sleeping with dogs. And, I had to admit, it was infinitely more satisfying.

"Mom! *Mom!*"

I heard Madison, our middle daughter, bounding down the stairs. What would get a thirteen-year-old up and out of bed so early — and on a Saturday? I went inside and nearly collided with her in her haste to get to the window. Up she clambered, onto the kitchen counter, and pressed her face against the glass.

"Are you okay?" I asked. "What's all the excitement?"

Nearly breathless, Madison turned to me, her face aglow with enthusiasm. "Do you know what *today* is?" she asked. "Do you?"

Well, of course I knew. It was the one-year anniversary of her father's death — we all knew that. Clearly, though, something else was on her mind. I decided to play dumb (which is, most days, not all that difficult to do).

"I give up," I said. "What's today?"

"Mom," Madison said reproachfully, swinging her long, colt-like legs off the counter and walking over to where I stood. "*Today* is the day Daddy died. I cannot believe you forgot."

I looked into Madison's face and saw no hint of confusion. She was serious — and yet her eyes sparkled, as though she knew a really good secret. Grabbing my hand, she pulled me back over to the counter and resumed her post at the window.

"Madison," I said slowly, choosing my words carefully, "what are we doing?"

"Look!" she insisted.

I looked. The driveway was empty. I wondered what she saw. A spirit? A vision of her father? God? (I knew I'd left Him out there, but I figured He might have followed me back into the house.) Was the child going crazy? Racking my brain for the name of a good psychiatrist who would take a teenager on short notice, I decided to play along.

"What am I looking at?" I asked.

"Nothing — yet," she chided. "They haven't come yet. But they will be here soon."

"Who will be here? It isn't even seven in the morning. Who is coming?"

"I don't know *which ones*, Mom, but they will *all* come."

Pouring myself another mug of coffee (and wondering if it was too early to think about switching to wine), I took a seat at the kitchen table. "Madison," I said gently, "please sit down and tell me what all of this is about."

"Okay," she agreed, pulling up a chair and propping her elbows on the table. "Today is the anniversary of Daddy's death, right?"

I nodded my head yes.

"Well, you said," she continued, in the patient-yet-exasperated tone of someone who thinks what they are explaining is blatantly obvious, "that after Daddy died it was the *proper* thing for our family to be in mourning for a year, because we are a *funeral* family and we are *Southern*, right?"

I nodded again, not sure where any of this was going, but glad she had her facts straight.

"Well, it has been a year and now we don't have to mourn anymore, right?"

Still not sure what I was supposed to say, I kept my mouth shut.

Taking a deep breath, Madison finally unleashed her thoughts: "All of the other single moms date, but you said you weren't allowed to date because you were in mourning. Well, it has been a year."

"Oh, honey." I sighed as the weight of understanding finally fell. "You are right. It *has* been a year. But all of the moms you know who date are divorced, and I am a widow, and that feels different somehow. I just don't think I am ready to date anyone. Your daddy and I were very much in love—"

"Mom!" Madison interrupted, her voice rising now. "It. Has. Been. A. Year!"

I looked at the clock. Not even 7:30 yet. It was going to be a long day.

Slowly, my daughter leaned forward, her face inches from mine. "Go upstairs," she said, clearly and deliberately, as though I was not only stupid but probably deaf too. "You look horrible. Put on some makeup and do your hair. And put on something with a little style."

When I hesitated, she grabbed my hands and pulled me out of my chair. "Hurry up!" she insisted. "They will be here soon!"

I scuttled up the stairs, wondering what had become of

my life. Being a widow was bad enough; being hounded by a fairy-godmother-of-a-daughter was awful. I closed the bathroom door, locking it behind me, lest she come in to check on my progress.

I took a critical look in the mirror. Madison had exaggerated. I didn't look *horrible*. Tired maybe. And not exactly twentysomething. But I still had nice legs, thanks partly to God and partly to my daily workouts. I leaned closer to the glass. Was that a new wrinkle? Maybe. But it was nothing that some mascara and a stiff shot of Botox couldn't fix. Sure, a funeral director had tools like duct tape and embalming fluid at his disposal (and I'd seen Johnnie work magic on some of our less attractive acquaintances), but a plastic surgeon—now *that* would be a good husband to have on call. *Maybe*, I thought as I rooted around for my eyebrow tweezers, *one of them would show up on the white horse of Madison's dreams.*

By lunchtime, I'd lost count of how many times Madison had gone outside to check the driveway, letting more flies in the house with each foray. "I just don't understand," she would wail every thirty minutes or so. "Has anyone *called*?"

"No," I would answer, reaching for the flyswatter for what seemed the millionth time, "no one has called."

By midafternoon, Madison had stopped peppering me with questions. Instead, she wandered into the kitchen at random intervals, muttering about my hair or saying something about my clothes before shaking her head and walking out of the room. I thought about calling a man—any man—to come over and just *pretend* to be interested in me, but I didn't know anyone who was single, at least not anyone I would trust to play the part. All of Johnnie's and my really good friends were married.

Finally, the dinner hour arrived. That boded well, since it meant two things — wine for me and an impending bedtime for the girls. Once the dishes were done, I announced that it was bath time. Jacquie and Aven, Madison's older and younger sisters, hustled up the stairs, arguing over who had dibs on my shower that night. Madison hung back, stealing one last glance out the window.

My hope, as I made my bedtime rounds — saying prayers, dispensing kisses, and tucking each daughter in for the night — was that Madison would be fast asleep by the time I got to her room. I had saved her for last, on purpose.

But her lights were still on. And when I peeked in her door, she was sitting upright in her bed, her arms crossed and her attitude bolstered by an army of stuffed animals, all of whom seemed to glare at me as though I'd made some sort of heinous and unforgivable mistake.

I slipped into the room and sat on the edge of the bed.

"I just don't get it," Madison said with a sigh, more defeated than angry now. "Why didn't anyone come to date you today? You look nice enough. I mean, you're not ugly or anything like that. You're really smart. And Daddy liked you a lot."

"Oh, Madison," I said, brushing the hair from her face, "God has a plan for us. He will take care of us. He never makes mistakes — never! He will provide someone for me to date when he knows the time is right — for me and for all of us."

I leaned back on the bed, feeling satisfied with my explanation and imagining that God was pleased with me too. I loved the idea that my daughter could learn from my example of faith and that she would be equipped to put her trust in God. Who needed a father when there was such a wise and insightful mother around to be such a good Christian role model? Maybe I really could do this single-parent thing after all.

I closed my eyes, picturing my daughters growing up to be strong women of faith. I was almost asleep when I felt a gentle pressure on my hand. Coming awake, I saw Madison's eyes peering earnestly into mine.

"So, what do you think you did wrong? You need to figure this out so it doesn't happen again ..."

Madison was still talking when I reached the door of her room. "Good night, darling," I said as I turned out the light.

PART
ONE

Life and Death
with Johnnie

Dating
the Grim Reaper

I watched, mesmerized, as the heat waves danced lazily on the blacktop of the hospital parking lot. If I squinted, I could almost pretend they were a mist rising up from the ocean, or some sort of desert mirage. It was hot as all get-out. I felt the sweat trickling down my chest, and I wondered, with a sort of morbid curiosity, what would happen if I just had a heat stroke and fell over.

Probably nothing. My family was too engrossed in their discussion to notice my discomfort. But weren't they hot too? Why didn't someone suggest we finish our conversation inside, where the cool, dark hush of the hospital lobby sanitized all feeling?

"She would definitely not want 'Amazing Grace,'" my aunt insisted. "I am not even sure she would want any singing."

"Yes, but —"

"And we can't have the reception at home, even if it is just family. Too confusing. Jacquie, can you call the Club?"

Snippets of conversation darted about like swallows in the air — *flowers, an obituary, the proper suit to wear.* My grandmother had just died. I felt the grief welling up inside me. I wanted to cry — but not about losing Momma Claire. I wanted to cry because I was so stinking hot, hot as Hades, and it didn't seem like anyone had any intention of leaving the sweltering parking lot. There was a funeral to plan, and no matter that it was to be just family and a few close friends, my mother — Jacquie Branch, the queen of everything — was gearing up for an *event*. Dress shopping had to be done, hair appointments booked, ham biscuits ordered. At the ripe old age of twenty-one, I could not have cared less. I loved my grandmother, but I didn't want to think about her funeral. I just wanted to go to the beach.

Finally, just as I thought I really might pass out, some sort of an accord was reached and I was, thankfully, released.

Perhaps I should have paid better attention — at least to the wardrobe discussion. Momma Claire was to be laid to rest at Forest Lawn, and as I slid out of the car at the cemetery, keeping my knees together as my mother had told me all good girls do, I felt my cousin's stare.

"*Seriously?*" she hissed. "You wore *blue*? Don't you know you are supposed to wear *black* to a funeral?"

I didn't — but I wasn't about to let on. "Why on earth would anyone wear black?" I replied. "It is hot as all get-out, probably a hundred degrees, and everyone knows black absorbs sun. I will be much more comfortable in this dress — and for your information, it isn't blue; it is *teal*. And it matches my eyes."

Standing at Momma Claire's graveside, I sensed my aunt at my elbow. "Dee, darling," she whispered, "that blue is quite … becoming … but I do think you might have worn something a little less … garden party."

"It's teal," I muttered.

"What?" My aunt leaned in, keeping her voice low so as not to distract the minister, who was saying something about ashes and dust.

"Teal. The dress is *teal*. But can we please focus on Momma Claire?"

Rebuffed, at least for the moment, my aunt stepped back, and we turned our attention to the service. It was a smallish gathering, and I was struck by how many employees from the funeral home seemed to be lurking about. Dressed in dark suits and red-and-navy-striped ties, they looked more like secret service men than undertakers. A couple of the guys looked familiar, which wasn't surprising. The H.D. Oliver Funeral Home had been in business for nearly two hundred years, and the Oliver family, like my own, had called Tidewater, Virginia, home since … well, since forever, I guess.

We bid farewell to Momma Claire — who, mercifully, was perhaps the only family member who did not weigh in on the color of my dress — and I didn't give another thought to the Olivers.

A week or so later, the phone rang. It was my cousin Vicki, wanting to know whether I might be willing to "meet someone."

I'd just ended a rather unremarkable relationship, and not

having anything better to do, I figured what the heck. "Sure," I said. "Set me up."

(Note to the single gal: Before agreeing to any blind date, get some background intel. The guy could turn out to be a serial killer. Worse still, he could work with people who are already dead. But I am getting ahead of myself.)

We set a date, and I drove the twenty-five minutes from my home in Virginia Beach to a neighborhood bar in Norfolk. Spying a spot right in front of the place (this date showed promise already!), I eased my jacked-up four-wheel-drive Chevy Blazer with the killer sound system into the parking space and cut the engine.

Vicki met me at the door, taking my elbow protectively as my eyes struggled to adjust to the dim lighting. "Okay," she said, "Mr. Wonderful is here."

"Whoa," I replied, halting in my tracks. "Let's get some info first. Like, what's his name?"

"John Oliver. He is thirty-five years old and — "

"Stop. You did not just say *thirty-five*. That is old. Way old. Like, older-than-dirt old."

"Oh, Dee," Vicki said with a laugh. "It's not *that* bad. And John is cute. He just got divorced and — "

"Vicki!" I pulled my arm out of her grasp. "No! Look at me, Vicki. Look me in the eye. N. O. No."

"Oh, come on, Dee. You know his family. It will be okay."

"I do?"

"Yes! He's one of the H.D. Olivers. You know — the funeral people."

This had to be some kind of sinister joke. I mean, who goes out with a funeral person? And do those people — I couldn't bring myself to even think the word *mortician* — even date?

I spun on my heel and was headed back toward the door when Vicki's sister came strolling up, her arm linked through the arm of one of the handsomest men I had ever seen.

"Hey, Dee Dee," she cooed, her smile breaking into a grin. "This is Johnnie. Vicki and I thought you might like to meet him."

Johnnie extended his hand, his blond hair falling loosely over one of his gorgeous brown eyes. I found my resistance softening — until I caught sight of his black pinstriped suit. It fairly shouted, "Death."

I wanted to bolt back to the Beach — and to the bevy of surfer boys I typically hung out with — but if Jacquie Branch had taught me nothing else, she taught me how to be a lady, and that included a fluency in small talk. I made a few polite remarks and then excused myself to visit the restroom. But even the most well-bred Southern charm has its limits, and I couldn't help myself. I had just met the Grim Reaper. Yes, he had nice eyes. But I don't even watch horror films. *Why, I asked myself, would I ever want to date one?* I passed the bathroom and headed straight for the exit.

Plus, I thought as I put the Blazer in gear, *that guy's on the verge of collecting Social Security.* Punching the radio button, I let the sound of Aretha Franklin belting out her need for a little R-E-S-P-E-C-T soar through my open windows as I sped home through the night.

Four months later, Vicki invited me to attend an art exhibit. Afterward, we headed to the same bar where I'd met Johnnie. "They have a great steak-and-fries dinner," she explained, knowing the way to my heart.

We had just polished off the last of the beef when who should come strolling through the door but Mr. Pinstriped Suit himself. I prayed that Johnnie wouldn't see me, but sure enough, he spotted our table and sauntered over, a gleam in his even-more-gorgeous-than-before brown eyes.

"Mind if I join you?" he asked, taking a chair.

Almost on cue, Vicki stood up, smiled, and said she was leaving. And to my horror she did — taking my exit strategy with her. Stranded in a less-than-upscale Norfolk neighborhood, I was savvy enough to know I wouldn't get very far without a car.

Undeterred by her departure, Johnnie ordered two beers — one for me — and began talking.

"I saw you at your grandmother's funeral," he said.

"At the cemetery?" I asked. "You noticed me *in a graveyard*?"

"Well," Johnnie said, laughing, "you were hard to miss. I loved the color of your dress. It matched your eyes."

Maybe it was the beer, but ten minutes later I found myself looking past the pinstriped suit. Twenty minutes later, our age difference didn't seem quite so stark.

"Okay, I'll be really honest," Johnnie said, leaning across the table. "When I spotted you that day, I asked one of my guys who you were. I figured they'd know — I mean, there are not that many girls in town who have legs like yours. In fact" — he smiled, a little sheepishly — "I think my exact words that day were, 'Who's the girl with the legs?' "

Mortified (and, okay, kind of flattered), I remembered that the blue dress — the *teal* dress — was not, actually, all that long. And it's not like I am boasting when I admit that God has, in fact, blessed me with a pretty decent set of gams. I found myself secretly happy that Johnnie had noticed.

We kept talking.

An hour later, I had made it past the fact that he was divorced. I was still not comfortable with the whole funeral director thing, but the fact that Johnnie was cute, smart, witty, and incredibly charming kept the visions of ghosts at bay. I agreed to go out with him again, this time on an "official" date.

My mother was ecstatic. She bought me three new outfits in anticipation of the evening; she knew Johnnie's family and, evidently, considered him quite a catch. When the doorbell rang, I opened the door and felt my knees go weak. Standing on the front porch in his blue blazer and khaki pants, with his shirt open at the collar, Johnnie was a transformed man. Without the death suit, he looked like a J.Crew model. (An older model, to be sure, but still ...)

Johnnie had made reservations at the Steak and Ale. We climbed into his 280z black sports car, five on the floor, and I thought to myself, *This guy is getting cuter by the minute.*

But then he broke the spell. "I'm on call tonight," he said. "I tried to get someone to cover for me, but no one could do it. But I am sure it won't be a problem. I hope you don't mind."

Mind? Why would I mind? I was on a date with a J.Crew model — and I didn't even know what being "on call" meant.

Two miles later, I found out. Johnnie's pager went off, and we pulled into the nearest 7-Eleven so he could use the pay phone.

"Ah, I have to make a quick house call," he explained, sliding back in behind the wheel. "It won't take but a minute. Do you mind?"

For the second time in as many minutes, I found myself saying I didn't mind, particularly since, like with "on call," I had no idea what a "house call" entailed. Plus, I was hungry, and I wasn't sure what else I would do for dinner if this date went south.

Before I knew what was happening, we'd pulled into the parking lot of the funeral home — which turned out to be Johnnie's actual home too — and he jumped out of the car, saying he just needed to "run in and change clothes." I was still processing the fact that my date lived among the dead (clearly we would not be coming back later for a nightcap), when Johnnie was back, decked out in that all-too-familiar pinstripe. Much to my surprise, he didn't get into the car; instead, he came around and opened my door.

"We need to switch cars," he explained, motioning toward a black station wagon.

I wasn't quite sure what to make of the swap, but I have always prided myself on being a good sport, and if nothing else, my curiosity was piqued. Trying to look unconcerned,

I adopted my best "it's cool" face, and we headed out into the night.

Ten minutes later, we pulled into a driveway. Through the windshield I could see two other men — pinstriped bookends in matching ties — standing on the lawn, apparently waiting for Johnnie to arrive. They surrounded the car and opened Johnnie's door, like maybe they expected to find the president driving. Johnnie turned to me, and I felt my heart flutter as a lock of his hair fell over his eye. "Don't go anywhere," he said. "I'll be right back."

Where would I go?

With nothing to do but wait, I lit up a Virginia Slims. Sitting in the darkened car, my smoke wafting out the open window, I pondered my plight. My date was old, divorced, and employed in a decidedly creepy job. Still, he was cute. And unpredictable. That, I thought, was probably a plus.

I stamped out my cigarette and heard a noise that sounded like someone had opened the station wagon's rear door. Before I could turn my head, I felt a jolt that knocked me forward in my seat. Had something smacked into the back of the car? I turned to look, and — lo and behold — I was no longer alone. There, a mere six inches from my elbow, was … a sheet. On some sort of a board. Or maybe it was a cot. Whatever it was, there was definitely something — or someone — underneath the white cloth.

"Okay," Johnnie said, sliding into the driver's seat, "we're done here. This is Mrs. Smith. I'm hungry and I bet you are too, so let's go get dinner."

For the first time I could ever remember, I was speechless. There I was, in a brand-new dress, sitting in a car in a strange neighborhood with a man who was not like anyone I'd ever met before. And a dead person.

Finally I found my voice. "Will Mrs. Smith be joining us for dinner?" I asked.

Johnnie laughed — a big, hearty, warm, and wonderful laugh — and right then, crammed into the front seat with a man I barely knew and a woman I never would, I knew the truth: *I was going to marry John Oliver.*

THE RING TOSS

*J*ohnnie and I had been dating for about six months, and to avoid the twenty-mile commute between Norfolk (where he lived and worked) and Virginia Beach (where I still lived in my parents' oceanfront home), I had taken to spending the night at Vicki's house more often than not. It was, I figured, better than spending the night in the funeral home — and not just because I wasn't the kind of girl who shacked up with her man. I also wasn't the kind of girl who fancied sleeping among the dead.

My college graduation was approaching, and I was looking forward to celebrating. My mother, having just had the first of several face-lifts, had missed my high school ceremony, but she was still looking pretty good four years later, and I figured she'd be up for some sort of party this time.

I figured wrong.

"Good news, Dee!" she announced one day out of the blue. "Your father's ship will be in Spain or Italy next month, and I've booked a trip for us."

"Next month?" I asked. "Mom, that's my graduation. I was kind of thinking I would attend that."

"Oh, don't be silly, dear. They can mail those diploma things. Let's go to Europe!"

I thought that one over. My father was a navy captain, and he seemed to always be somewhere in Europe. Mom was forever jetting off to meet him in one port or another; a trip to Italy or Spain did not seem, to me, to be grounds for skipping one of life's major milestones.

"I think I'd rather not," I said. "I don't really want to go to Europe."

"Well, all right then," Mom said brightly. "I know what we'll do. Your father and I will send you to *Bermuda*! On a *cruise*! It will be a *graduation* present! You can leave right out of Norfolk, and you can take Vicki with you.

"Call the school," she continued, warming to her new plan. "Get them to send you your diploma. And when we all get back, we shall have a wonderful celebration!"

And just like that, it was settled.

I had no real desire to go to Bermuda — or anywhere else, for that matter — but my darling mother was bound for Europe and I was going wherever and whenever she sent me, even if it meant missing my own graduation ceremony. Thus it was that, three weeks later, I found myself kissing Johnnie good-bye (he'd been kind enough to drive Vicki and me to the dock) and promising I'd be back in ten short days.

As it turned out, they were ten *long* days. Maybe it was because the Bermuda plan was formulated so late in the game, or maybe it was because she'd spent most of her money on luxury hotels in Spain and Italy, but my mother had booked us into the very worst room on the entire ship. It was windowless, with a bathroom so small that the entire room got wet when you took a shower, including the towels. At night, when the lights were out, the darkness seemed to press in on every side. I lay there on the top bunk (yes, Vicki and I had bunk beds) and found myself thinking about Johnnie a lot and wondering if this was how it felt to be in one of his caskets.

When the ship returned to port, Johnnie waited at the end of the gangway. Never in my wildest imaginings had I thought I would be so happy to see a pinstriped undertaker! And when we got in his black car and he filled me in on the lives and deaths of the recently deceased, along with all the details of their services, I found myself captivated.

That night, Johnnie picked me up for dinner. "Hey," he said, "open the glove box. There is something in there for you."

I reached in and pulled out a half-eaten candy bar.

"Um — thank you," I said. "But can I save this for after dinner?"

"No, no," Johnnie said, laughing, "not that. That's my candy. Reach farther in, toward the back."

I did, and my hand closed around a small, square leather box.

"Oh, my." I pulled it out and felt my heart leap into my throat.

Johnnie continued to drive, his eyes on the road. "I didn't

realize how much you meant to me until you were gone. I really missed you. So ..."

He seemed to be fishing for words as I sat there looking at the box and wondering what was inside.

"So go ahead," he finally said. "Open it!"

I lifted the lid, and there, nestled against a cushion of Tiffany velvet, was the biggest, most beautiful diamond ring I had ever seen. Sparkling in the reflection of the dashboard lights — Bruce Springsteen was on the radio, singing some song about the USA — the diamond seemed to light up the whole car.

"Do you like it?" Johnnie asked.

"Yes! I love it!"

"Good."

And that was it.

Johnnie drove on in silence. I studied the ring, wondering what the heck he had meant by "Good." Had I just been proposed to? It sure looked like an engagement ring, but with Prince Charming behind the wheel of his black funeral car instead of atop a white horse, I wasn't quite sure. I mean, where was the bended knee? The romance? The princess story?

Finally, I couldn't stand the suspense. "Johnnie," I said, "what, exactly, is this ring?"

"It's for you."

He'd already made that clear. The candy bar was his; the ring was mine. I was beginning to feel like he'd been taking conversation lessons from some of his clients — the silent ones.

34

"What are you giving it to me for?"

"I thought we would get married. Would you like to?"

"So are you proposing to me?"

"Yes. Can't you tell that?"

"No. You haven't asked me."

"Well, I gave you a ring. So would you?"

I realized this ping-pong exchange was probably as romantic as this conversation was going to get, so I said yes. Johnnie kept driving, Bruce kept singing, and just like that, I was engaged.

My mother, of course, took full credit for the match. "You see?" she said. "This would never have happened if your father and I hadn't sent you on that trip to Bermuda. That's when Johnnie knew he couldn't live without you!"

I grudgingly admitted she was probably right, but if she expected me to write her some sort of thank-you note for sticking Vicki and me in a windowless cubby for ten days while the postman delivered my college diploma to an empty house, well, that wasn't going to happen. I was, however, grateful for her can-do spirit when it came to wedding planning.

Like all mothers who have daughters, I guess, my wedding became "hers," and Jacquie Branch was in her element. It didn't matter that we had less than six months to pull it all off (Johnnie and I had set a date for September, and I think my mother was secretly glad it would be upon us so soon, lest he change his mind); she went to work with a light in her eyes that I hadn't seen since US Air had introduced its direct-to-New York flight that set travelers back a mere $35. Parties were in full swing; the church had been booked, the country club ballroom reserved, and the wedding dress ordered (as befitting Johnnie's and my romance, the train seemed to stretch all the way from Virginia Beach to Norfolk); and all manner of silver, crystal, and pieces from two china patterns arrived daily at our house via UPS. Throw in the parade of bridesmaids — I had settled on eleven — and my mother was in nuptial heaven.

Johnnie, however, was not.

He was, as it turned out, down the street drinking martinis.

It was a month or so before the wedding, and Johnnie was due to pick me up for a dinner date we had booked with some friends. He was normally a punctual fellow, so now, as the minutes ticked into hours, I grew concerned. Perhaps someone had died. I'd been dating Johnnie long enough to know that death pretty much trumps everything in a funeral director's life, and this wouldn't be the first time we'd had to put our plans on hold. Surely, though, he would have called.

Two hours after he should have been there, my worry had given way to anger. John Oliver had not yet met my temper, but unless he was dead himself, there was a good chance he'd see it tonight. That is, if he ever showed up.

Why hadn't he called?

Kicking off my sandals, I sunk into Vicki's La-Z-Boy recliner and silently fumed. When the doorbell rang, I leapt up and flung open the door. There was Johnnie, looking as drop-dead handsome as ever, wearing a sheepish grin.

"Where have you — "

I caught a whiff of Johnnie's breath and stopped short. Had he been drinking? He had! And, from what I could tell, he was smashed.

"Please tell me," I began softly, "that somebody died in a bar. And that once you removed him, the family convinced you to stay for a drink."

"No," Johnnie slurred, still smiling. "I stopped off at Mike's house for a quick martini, and guess who was there?"

"I haven't a clue," I said, keeping my temper in check, "but please do tell me, because you are two hours late."

"It was Sue, the girl I dated before you!"

He said it like I would be happy, like he had won some sort of contest.

"You are kidding me, right?" I was too young to know much about blood pressure, but I was pretty sure mine was starting to spike. "I have been sitting here, dressed and ready for dinner, *for two hours*, and our friends have gone on without us, while you have been drinking with *an old girlfriend*?"

Johnnie considered this. "Well, now," he said, "it sounds kinda bad when you say it like that."

"I can't believe you!" I shouted, throwing to the wind every how-to-be-a-lady lesson I'd ever learned. Visions of dark suits and headstones clouded my eyes, and I thought about how good it would feel to pop the tailgate on one of H.D. Oliver's "removal wagons" and shove Johnnie's body in, headfirst.

Sensing the storm that was upon him, Johnnie tried to protest, saying that the wedding had "put him under a lot of pressure."

"Then let me help you remove some of that pressure," I said. I twisted the ring off my finger — the one-carat diamond offered a ready handle — and clenched it in my fist. Johnnie probably thought I was going to hit him, but I'd backed off and was too far away for that. Instead, from a distance of about fifteen feet, I cocked back my elbow and let the missile fly.

It was the perfect throw, one I couldn't repeat in a thousand tries.

Johnnie's mouth was open — undoubtedly to offer some other lame excuse — and the ring hit him square in the back of the throat. He looked at me, stunned, and then he began to gasp and choke.

Good! I thought, as I watched his eyes grow wide. But when he began to turn a pale shade of blue, I figured I'd better do something. I didn't care if he died; I just didn't want him to do it in Vicki's Norfolk apartment.

I crossed the room and came behind Johnnie, circling his body with my arms and thrusting my fists below his rib cage while squeezing upward as I'd been taught to do in the mandatory first-aid class I'd taken in college.

I thought surely I'd break a rib but, sadly, that wasn't the case. Instead, Johnnie let loose a mighty cough, and the ring tumbled out of his mouth and onto Vicki's hardwood floor. We both stared at it as though it might jump up and attack again.

Finally, Johnnie bent over, picked it up, and shoved it into his pocket. "If that is what you think of my ring," he slurred, "I will just go on and keep it."

He hadn't even thought to thank me for saving his life. "That's fine," I said, through gritted teeth. "You can keep your old ring."

And he did.

The next morning I drove over to my parents' house. My mother was in the dining room, surrounded by a sea of Wedgwood's Kutani Crane (the multiple colors, my mother had explained, would go with any table décor) and Lismore goblets by Waterford (identical to the ones she owned so that, as she artfully put it, I could "look forward" to inheriting hers, knowing they would all match). We had not even mailed the invitations yet, and already our dining room looked like a Fifth Avenue window display.

"Look, darling, the invitations arrived!" She held a stack of white cards triumphantly in her right hand. "They are absolutely *perfect!*"

I let my gaze drift to the window, unwilling to shatter her joy just yet. It was August, and I could see the ocean just beyond the fence line of my parents' manicured lawn. I pictured my friends sitting out there on the beach, unencumbered by a department store's worth of now-unwanted crystal goblets and Tiffany silver. I hadn't thought too much about God since my graduation from Catholic high school more than four years earlier; now I found myself silently praying that my mother wouldn't faint when I told her my news. Either that, or maybe God could just open up a crater in the dining room floor and swallow me whole, taking a whole dinner party's worth of china and flatware with me.

"Mom, John and I have had an argument."

"No worries, darling." My mother smiled. "These things happen. It will be fine."

"No, Mother, it will not be fine."

"Yes, it will," she replied, more firmly this time. "I've seen it happen a thousand times before. It's just wedding jitters. These things always work themselves out."

"No," I said again, taking a tentative step toward her. "The wedding is off. We are not getting married."

There. I'd said it. The dining room floor didn't open, and my mother was still upright. Both were, I thought, good signs.

My mother did not speak. I waited. Still, she stood there. *Can people die standing up?* I wondered. Finally, I saw her blink. Clearly, she was not dead. I moved closer.

"Mom?" I began, softly. "Did you hear m — "

"Oh my God!" My mother's scream rattled the plates. I jumped back, fearful that she might actually explode, or flip the table or something.

My father, recently returned from his umpteenth voyage, barged into the room like a torpedo. "What on earth is going on?" he demanded to know.

"Your daughter has called off the wedding!"

Dad's gaze shifted from my mother's stricken face to mine. "What happened?"

Slowly I filled them in on Johnnie's infidelity. No matter that he hadn't slept with, or even kissed, his old girlfriend; knocking back martinis with her while I waited, all dressed up and all alone, signaled, I thought, an irreparable character flaw.

"I don't want to marry him," I said. "It's over."

My mother sank to the floor, collapsing amid a pile of boxes, white tissue paper, and engraved envelopes, and began to cry.

"Jacquie," my father began calmly, his captain's demeanor bringing order amid the wreckage, "if the girl doesn't want to marry the boy, we are not going to make her marry him."

Sensing my opportunity, I slipped out of the room to let my parents talk. I moved outside. I could hear my mother wailing through the open windows and wondering how in the world she was going to explain "all this" to her friends. Finally, I felt my father's presence at my side.

"Honey," he said, "I am taking your mother to Florida. I think it is best. Let me know if you need anything."

The next day they were gone. I returned the gifts, threw away the invitations, and sent Johnnie the bill for my dress, along with the bills for the eleven we'd purchased for the bridesmaids.

A week passed. My father called with regular updates; my mother, it seemed, was inconsolable. I went back to the life I'd known the summer before: sipping Coronas on the beach, hanging out with my friends, and checking out the surfer boys. Saying good-bye to a mortician was, I figured, no great loss. Maybe I should aim higher next time. Maybe I should date a doctor . . .

Southern
Princess Weds
Mr. Pinstriped Suit

*T*wo years after what my family euphemistically referred to as "the ring toss," I was still unengaged, unemployed (unless you count a string of part-time jobs that didn't make my father feel very good about the money he'd invested in my education), and having the time of my life. I had, in fact, found my doctor-boyfriend, but he turned out to have a bad habit of writing illegal prescriptions, and even before he landed in a cinder-block cell I realized the relationship didn't show much promise. I'd also been engaged — briefly — to a dashing young fighter pilot, but when we broke up and he ditched the classic, "It's not you; it's me" line in favor of the less common, "It *is* you — you are *such* a princess!" line, I knew it never would have worked with that guy. We were both prima donnas.

I'd been sponging off my parents, living in their now-vacant beach house. My father had retired from the navy and taken a lucrative job with an investment firm, and they'd moved to North Miami Beach. Florida had the added plus, I knew, of serving as a safe harbor for my fugitive mother, who still couldn't face her social circle after the horror of "the toss." She'd be happy to move back to Virginia Beach, she implied, after all her friends were dead.

Johnnie and I had kept in touch. We met every once in a while for dinner or drinks, and while I would sooner have died than admit it to him, he still had the power to stop me in my tracks. Thus it was that he was the one person I called with the news that life, as I knew it, was about to come to a screeching halt.

"Hey, Johnnie," I said when he picked up the phone.

"Hey, yourself."

Just hearing his voice made me feel better about my predicament. "I'm just calling to let you know I'm taking a job in Florida."

"What? What job?"

"Well, I don't really know what job, exactly. But my father called today and said I had to be productive in a 'What can a girl with a private college education do for the world?' kind of way."

"But you don't know what job?" Johnnie was nothing if not practical, and he wanted some specifics.

"Not really. I mean, it's nine-to-five and all, and it comes with things like health care and dental and a real office. And lunch. Dad set it all up for me. He says they'll expect me to show up five days a week, and that they'll give me something I haven't had in a while — a paycheck."

"When are you leaving?" Johnnie asked.

"Soon, I gather. They are sending me a plane ticket. But …"

"But what?" Johnnie wanted to know.

"But Mom got on the phone after Dad finished talking to me and said I didn't need to worry about the job if I didn't like it. Apparently, she has three very handsome, very wealthy South American men for me to meet, and she feels sure one of them will suit. So it seems I am either going to be employed or auctioned off to the highest bidder."

Johnnie didn't say anything.

"Hello?" I said.

"I'm here," he said. "It's just that — well, you're kidding, right?"

"I wish. But no. My dad is pretty serious. Mom too."

"Okay." Johnnie paused, and let out a breath. "Then let's get married."

"What?" I wasn't sure I'd heard him right. (And even if he was asking what I thought he was, it occurred to me that he hadn't learned much about crafting a marriage proposal in the two years since I'd hit a ringer on his tonsils with my hole in one.)

"Let's get married," he repeated. "I still have the ring."

"You do?" I said, not sure whether I could believe him. Hanging on to an expensive ring for two years — particularly one that had nearly served as a murder weapon — didn't make a lot of sense to me. But it *was* kind of romantic. "Where is it?" I asked.

"In the family safe."

I'd seen the safe; it was a gigantic black box set on wheels, probably about seven feet tall and four feet wide, emblazoned with gold letters that read, "H.D. Oliver." It lived — along with seemingly everything that mattered to Johnnie — at the funeral home, and it appeared designed to withstand an atom bomb. I'd never thought (or wanted) to ask what they kept in the safe; now, evidently, I knew.

"Okay, then," I heard myself say, as visions of South American men and stacks of paychecks that I didn't want to have to earn vanished from my mind. "Let's get married."

Almost before I'd hung up the phone, Johnnie was at my door, ring in hand. "Let's go down to the Clerk of the Court," he said.

I didn't mind passing on the gifts and invitations — I'd been down that path before — but I knew I couldn't marry Johnnie without my parents' knowledge. I'd have their blessing, of that I was certain, but they'd probably want to be present at the ceremony, if for no other reason than to make sure it actually happened. I explained this to Johnnie, who offered an immediate solution: "We'll go to Florida."

I called my mother, who was, not surprisingly, ecstatic. "Deon!" she yelled into my ear, calling my father to the phone. "Your daughter is getting married!"

"To whom?"

"John! To John! She is going to marry John!"

"Now, darling," she said, turning her attention back to me, "I want you to go to the Naivete store in town and buy yourself a beautiful dress and a trousseau and have it all shipped here, to Tower Two." (My parents had traded in their sprawling oceanfront lifestyle for the urban chic of apartment living.) "Stop by the jewelers too, and pick up the wedding bands. I will take care of everything down here — see you soon!"

A week or so later, Johnnie and I headed to Florida. The trousseau had been shipped, and the wedding bands engraved with the date of our wedding: September 8, 1984.

"Darling!" Mother cried, throwing her arms wide to welcome us. "Your father has arranged for you to stay in *the penthouse*! I thought you'd want an extra day to honeymoon, so we've moved the wedding up a day. Isn't it all just so exciting?"

Johnnie couldn't take time off for an extended honeymoon (or, as I was soon to discover, to do much of anything), so my mother, in an effort to help us make the most of our forty-eight-hour getaway, had rescheduled the wedding for Friday rather than Saturday — as in, the Saturday that had been carved into our rings. The date change wouldn't matter much to the handful of guests who had heard about the wedding over drinks or bridge tables earlier that week; they were simply glad to be included in what promised, under my mother's extravagant hand, to be a lavish and memorable party.

"Did you get a minister?" I asked.

"Oh, no, Dee darling," my mother assured me. "They are much more easygoing down here. All you need is a notary public."

"Do we know any notaries?" I wondered aloud.

"Of course! Benjamin, the security guard who works downstairs in the lobby, is a notary. He can perform the ceremony."

Benjamin, like most of the residents in Tower Two (along with the two strangers my mother pressed into service as our token "witnesses"), was Jewish. That didn't appear to matter to Johnnie (a Catholic) or to my parents (Episcopalians), and I certainly was in no position to protest. I hadn't been to church since Christmas, but from what I knew about God, he seemed to be a pretty open-minded guy. Plus, weren't the Jews his favorites? I hadn't learned all that much about the Bible in my parochial school days, but I was pretty sure Jesus had been a Jew. And if my notary-minister was too, well then, that was all right by me.

We made it through the ceremony, drank way too much of my mother's special-order champagne, retired to the penthouse for the rest of the weekend, and began to live happily ever after.

It wasn't until a year or so later, as I was looking through our wedding pictures, that I noticed the Bible, which had been hastily borrowed from a neighbor just prior to the ceremony. There, in the classic photograph of the bride and groom's hands (ours, of course, wearing post-dated rings), was the black leather of the book. And right in between our fingers, in the place where I expected to see a gold, engraved cross, was the Star of David.

Well, I thought, *we are now complete — a Catholic, an Episcopalian, and a marriage blessed by the Jews. No matter what lies ahead, at least we have all our bases covered!*

From Caskets
to Cradles

*J*ohnnie and I had been married for a number of years,
and I was ready to start a family. I was more than ready,
in fact. Being around the dead and dying was not a bad
gig, but my friends were all getting pregnant and I found my
thoughts drifting more toward cradles than caskets. I pictured
our home filled with a whole gang of little Dee and Johnnie
look-alikes. Plus, Johnnie wasn't getting any younger, and I
wanted him to be able to push our children when we went out
for a walk rather than the other way around.

For years, our family planning had taken a back seat to
Johnnie's work. I didn't begrudge Johnnie the time he spent
at the funeral home; both his father and his brother had died
unexpectedly and within forty days of each other, and the loss
had rocked his world, both emotionally and professionally.
He'd been forced to step into shoes he hadn't yet planned to
wear. Thankfully, the boys who worked at H.D. Oliver — they
were men, really, but they were closer to Johnnie and to each

other than most brothers are, and I always thought of them as "the boys" — stepped into the gaps, and under Johnnie's steady leadership, the business continued to grow. Now I was ready to see our family do the same.

Happily, Johnnie seemed to be on board with my plan. Like most husbands, I guess, he loved the idea of "trying" to have children, and it seemed he was ready to try again almost every night. And when the pregnancy tests I brought home from the drugstore every month turned up negative, that didn't dampen his enthusiasm. "We'll just have to try a little harder!" he'd say with a smile, lifting my chin with his finger and slipping his arm around my waist.

I wanted to share his optimism, but as month after month went by and I continued to fail the tests — no college class had ever been this challenging — I grew more and more discouraged. "Cheer up," Johnnie would say, as though I could somehow dry my tears by sheer willpower. "There's always next month."

I had learned to depend on Johnnie, and I felt safe with him. Now, though, I felt like I was up against a problem that even he couldn't fix. With nowhere else to turn, I began to pray. After all, if babies came from heaven — and I was pretty sure they did — it just made sense to place an order with The Boss. (I didn't see it as being much different from asking Nordstrom to send over a new pair of black pumps.)

Unfortunately, it seemed that babies — or at least *my* baby — was on back order.

When the time came for my annual checkup, I told the doctor I had been trying to get pregnant.

"For how long?" he asked.

I turned the question over in my mind. It seemed we had been working pretty hard for the past year and a half, but — I sat up as the full realization hit me — I had stopped taking The Pill four years earlier.

"Hmmm." The doctor pondered this disclosure. "Why don't we go ahead and schedule a small surgery — just exploratory, nothing major — so I can look around and make sure there isn't anything else going on that we can't see."

Surgery? I must have nodded my head, because before I knew it, I was making an appointment with the secretary, but I was in shock. What could be going on in my body? What if there was something truly wrong and I'd never be able to have a baby?

Numb, I drove to the funeral home, where I knew I would find Johnnie. Sure enough, he was in the back office, surrounded by five of the boys, dressed all alike. They'd been discussing the funerals of the week, but when I stepped into the room and burst into tears, all conversation stopped. Six handkerchiefs came my way, like a flock of white birds. Funeral directors are nothing if not prepared for a good cry.

"Sweetheart," Johnnie said, stepping toward me, "what on earth is the matter?"

I told him what the doctor had said — that there might be something wrong with me, that maybe I couldn't get pregnant. With that, the boys all turned and looked at Johnnie, like maybe he was hiding a baby behind his back.

"Honey," he said, "I need to talk to you. Let's go up front to one of the family rooms."

The family rooms, I knew, were designed to let people grieve in peace, or talk quietly among themselves when making plans or decisions. Tastefully decorated, they signaled importance, seriousness, and — H.D. Oliver hoped — a sense of security that would keep fear and uncertainty at bay.

The boys stood mute, letting us pass. Johnnie guided me down the long hallway, the silence broken only by my intermittent sniffling.

"Sit here, honey." He patted the sofa and closed the door. "I want to talk to you."

"I'm scared," I said. "I don't want to have surgery. I just want to have a baby. What about adoption? Do you think we could adopt a baby? The doctor says — "

"Dee," Johnnie said, trying to stem the tide of my grief. I kept babbling.

"Dee!" he said, with more force than I thought the situation warranted. "Stop talking!"

"What?" I blew my nose into one of the handkerchiefs and looked at him.

"When are they talking about doing surgery?" he asked.

"In two days. They had a cancellation, so I was able to get right in." The very thought brought a fresh wave of tears, and I began to sob in earnest.

"Whoa," Johnnie said. "I think you should cancel it."

"I know. I don't want to have the operation. But I just want to get it over with. I want to know what's wrong! I — "

"Dee." Johnnie's voice was softer now. "I have to tell you something."

I let the handkerchief drop to my mouth, willing myself to listen.

Johnnie reached up and took one of my hands in his. *Please, God*, I thought, *don't let him tell me he doesn't want children, or that we can't adopt.*

"A long time ago," he began, "before I met you, I had a vasectomy."

A *what*? I closed my eyes as my mind struggled to process the word: Vasectomy. *Vasectomy!* What the —

My eyes flew open, and I let go of Johnnie's hands.

"Let me explain!" he said, his words tumbling out in a flood. "I had a vasectomy — yes — but it was years ago and I didn't want to tell you because I was — I mean I *am* — so very much in love with you and I knew you would never marry me if you knew."

I wanted to interrupt, but I couldn't find the words — and clearly, Johnnie wasn't finished.

"I just couldn't stand to lose you," he said. "I thought if we got married, we could just work it out later."

Vasectomy. Vasectomy. I rolled the word around in my mind, grasping for some sort of response.

"Say something, honey," Johnnie begged. "Say anything."

I looked into his brown eyes and felt something break inside of me. I couldn't tell if it was my heart or the dam that held my temper in check. "Do you know," I said, slowly, "that it is illegal to enter into a marriage knowing you cannot have children and not telling your fiancée that?"

He thought about that for a second or two. "Well, yeah. I guess."

"John," I said, standing up as I felt the heat rise inside of me, "I have just one thing to say to you."

"Yes?" he asked.

"Get a lawyer, boy, because you are going to need one."

With that, I flung open the door, and the boys — all five of them — practically toppled into the room. They had been listening to our every word!

"Johnnie?" I asked, turning back to stare at him. "Did *they* know about your … operation?"

The silence hung so heavy that, had we not already been among the dead, you would have thought we were. That answered my question. I glared at the boys, and they took off, running for their very lives down the hall to take refuge in the embalming room. Perhaps they thought they were safe there, but my quarrel was not with them. I stormed out of the building and headed for home.

I wanted to break something — anything — but I knew I would have to clean up the mess. I wanted to throw Johnnie's clothes on the front lawn, but I didn't want to give the neighbors the satisfaction of literally seeing our dirty laundry (and then talking about it for years). I wanted to kill Johnnie, to get the boys to shove him into the cremator just like the witch in "Hansel and Gretel," but even as I contemplated the plan, I knew I couldn't bring myself to do it. I would end up in jail. And I have never worn orange all that well.

What to do, what to do? I sat down on the sofa, then got up to pace. I considered my options. I wanted to kill Johnnie, yes, but I really did love him. I couldn't imagine living without him. But I wanted children. My own children. I didn't want to adopt. And if I stayed married to Johnnie and we didn't have children, I would end up hating him and the marriage would eventually fail. I had to divorce him. I didn't want to do it, but I couldn't see any other way.

Oh, God, I thought, *what just happened?* I sat down on the sofa again, my thoughts forming themselves into a prayer: *Help.*

You would think that, after twelve years of Catholic school and endless trips to the Episcopal Church for things like weddings and baptisms and Easter, I would know something about how to pray. "Bless us, O Lord, in these thy gifts — " No. That one was for before meals.

"Most merciful God …" I tried again, but couldn't remember what came next.

I knew how to pray the Hail Mary — and it seemed appropriate, given the whole motherhood thing — but I felt like a fraud, since I wasn't Catholic. Besides, I needed to go straight to the top.

I dropped to my knees and bowed my head. "Oh, God," I said, "I don't know what to do. I love Johnnie. You know I do. But I want to have a baby. Please, if you can do anything …"

I wasn't sure whether or not God had heard my prayer, or if I had even done it right. But when I stood up, I had to admit I felt better. If nothing else, I was glad I had called in some backup. When — or if — Johnnie ever came home, I figured I would need it.

He arrived home early and seemed surprised to find me

still there. "I am so sorry," he started. "Please forgive me. Please don't leave me."

"Oh, Johnnie, I'm sorry too. And I love you. But if we stay together, I will only wind up hating you, and I will probably hate myself too. It's better if we just end it now."

"Look," Johnnie said, "I have a plan. I just need some time. I called this doctor today and made an appointment to get it reversed. Will you please just wait long enough to see if this will work?"

I agreed, against my better judgment, but knowing I didn't have a choice. I loved him too much not to at least let him try. I later found out the odds of the operation working were about one in a million — the doctor made that clear, particularly since Johnnie's vasectomy was, like, the first one ever done, and nobody operated with an eye to a possible future reversal back then. "But," the doctor said, "you just never know about these things."

No, I thought, *I guess you don't*. But I knew Someone who did — or at least, I was getting to know him. I began talking to God every day, reminding him about Johnnie's situation and asking him to please "fix it." And I wasn't the only one praying. Always intensely private about his faith ("Christians and Jews, Muslims and Buddhists — we all need burying," he'd say, when asked about his religious beliefs), Johnnie admitted to me that he had taken to praying himself, in the quiet moments during the funerals he worked.

The time finally came for the test run, and the pressure was on. It was June 1991.

Jacqueline Alexander Oliver was born ten months later, in April 1992.

Madison Branch Oliver came into the world in 1994, with Aven Sterling Oliver following on her heels a scant sixteen months later.

"Please!" Johnnie begged. "Please, can we stop?"

"Gladly!" I smiled, surrounded by my three darling girls. "In fact, your birthday is coming up. How about if I treat you to a vasectomy?"

Johnnie loved that idea.

And I loved Johnnie. Our house was full, our prayers had been answered, and I didn't think I could be any happier.

WEEKEND
GETAWAY

*B*abies have a way of changing every marriage, and ours was no exception. During the barrenness of our vasectomy years, I'd grown very comfortable working at the funeral home. Johnnie's "boys" had become like brothers to me, and I enjoyed their company. Plus, having a woman on hand to walk alongside the bereaved as they processed everything from choosing a casket to writing an obituary certainly hadn't hurt business. Ours was, I will admit, a fairly loose arrangement; I showed up whenever Johnnie needed help and, in a compensation structure that satisfied us both, he paid me in shoes. As a result, two things happened: First, I wound up with about a hundred pairs of black pumps, and second, I discovered that I actually *liked* my job. I loved being with Johnnie during the day, and it felt good to know I really was helping the families that walked through our doors.

Then came motherhood. Suddenly, all of my knowledge about things like cremation and headstones was all but worthless as I struggled to learn a new language that revolved around words like *binky* and *potty training*, and where "pump" was no longer a shoe style so much as it was a breast-feeding strategy. The boys clearly wanted no part of my chaotic new life. "Stay home!" they commanded. "A funeral home is no place for babies or pregnant women. It's just not safe. Too many chemicals."

Truth be told, it didn't feel all that "safe" at home either. Oh, the babies were fine (unless you count the fact that Daughter #2 had an eye that had a bad habit of wandering away from the other one, which meant she was scheduled for surgery), but I felt like I was under attack. Three children under the age of four meant that our home ran on a single volume: *loud*. Gone were the days when I'd dream about repainting the kitchen (or even cleaning it); instead, I had begun to regard formula bottles as "décor." And I'd definitely lowered my personal beauty-and-hygiene standards. A good day was one on which I brushed my teeth, and a really good day was one on which I actually got dressed. It didn't matter whether I wore pajamas or Prada; I almost always smelled faintly like spit-up. If Johnnie hadn't already had his second vasectomy, I knew we'd still be okay on the birth control front. That boy wasn't about to come anywhere near me.

Johnnie's world remained unchanged. He'd leave home early in the morning and come home late at night, looking dashing and fit and exceptionally well rested after a long day at the office. I knew, based on my regular trips to places like the grocery store and the pediatrician's office, that there were a *lot* of people walking and driving around town, and that all of them were most definitely alive. Johnnie's oft-repeated claim that "people were dying" and that they all "needed him" began to sound a bit suspect. I mean, how many dead people could there really be? Johnnie had it backward. The bereaved didn't need *him*; he needed *them* — as an excuse to get away from us. From me.

To his credit, Johnnie recognized that my world was beginning to split at the seams. He walked in one night — dazzling in his pinstriped suit — and fixed himself a martini. He turned from the bar and took in the sight of my matted head (I hadn't found the brush that day), the kitchen counter littered with baby bottles, and a baby on my hip as I stirred our umpteenth chicken dinner on the stove. I don't know whether he'd thought it through or made a spur-of-the moment decision, but he raised his glass and — half shouting so as to be heard above the cacophony of crying children — announced, "We are going to take a short vacation."

"What?" I hollered back, not sure if I'd heard him right. "Tell me more!"

"I think we need to get you cleaned up," he said. "How about if we go to DC? We can stay at the Ritz for the weekend and have a real dinner." (I thought my growing culinary familiarity with chicken might be considered evidence of a real dinner, but I wasn't about to interrupt.)

"We'll sleep in, go sightseeing, do some shopping ..."

It sounded like heaven to me. "I will line up the babysitter!" I shouted, partly to be sure Johnnie heard me but mostly because I was so excited. I could smell the chicken burning now, but that didn't matter anymore. A real dinner was coming my way.

We made our plans, and as the day drew near, I could barely contain my excitement. I would get to wear makeup again! And real clothes!

But I'd been in the funeral business long enough to know that death is nothing if not unpredictable. Knowing that someone's untimely departure could derail our plans, I thought it would help if I reminded God that Johnnie and I would be on vacation. I began to pray that no one would die.

Normally, we prayed for death—I mean, not any *particular* death, but knowing that God is always updating the roster in heaven, I wasn't above asking him to consider H.D. Oliver as the best third party to assist with the send-off. But not if we were trying to leave town. In that case, it was best if nobody died. "Could you, God, maybe focus on *birth* for a few days," I hinted, eyeing the calendar, "and hold off on the whole *homecoming* thing?"

Sure enough, we hadn't gotten any calls, and all was right with the world. The babysitter was lined up; the children were healthy and happy; and our construction project (as if the chaos of our lives didn't provide enough stimulation, we'd made the young-and-dumb decision to break ground on a new house) was coming in on time and under budget. It was the perfect time to get away.

But then it happened.

"Honey," Johnnie said, calling me from the office a few

hours before we were due to leave, "don't get upset. I have it all worked out."

"What happened?" I asked, even though I knew what he'd say.

"Mrs. Thomas Jefferson died."

"Oh, no!" I cried, knowing the woman he spoke of (who was not, obviously, *the* Mrs. Thomas Jefferson). "I loved her. But" — and I am not proud of this next part — "couldn't she wait forty-eight hours? I mean, it's not like she would notice. She's not *sick*; she's just *dead*."

Johnnie laughed. "Don't worry," he said. "We're still going. As it turns out, Mr. Thomas Jefferson is buried in Arlington National Cemetery, and we can do the service up there on Saturday — "

"No!" I protested. "No, John! I am not going to a cemetery. You said we were going to the *mall*."

Johnnie kept talking, as though he hadn't heard me. "I thought we could take the hearse up there with her, and we'd spend the night at the Ritz and in the morning just drive over for the funeral. Then, as soon as it's over, we can go to the mall and have a nice lunch."

Oh. My. God. Was he hearing this? "John," I said, struggling to maintain my composure, "I am not — do you hear me? — *not* taking Mrs. Thomas Jefferson to the Ritz Carlton. I am not — again, do you hear me? — taking the *hearse* to the Ritz.

"And besides," I continued, my voice rising with every word, "there is no room for my luggage when that vehicle is loaded up with a casket and all the flowers. Where is my suitcase supposed to go? Strapped to the top? Now *that's* classy!"

Johnnie didn't miss a beat. "I will have the valet back the hearse into the garage so no one will bother Mrs. Jefferson. The car will be fine, and she will be fine."

Valet? Hearse? This scene was getting more bizarre by the minute. I could just picture the poor parking attendant, trying to smile but wanting to run, as Mr. and Mrs. Addams Family pulled up to his hotel.

"Johnnie, we can't —"

"Just think about all the room we'll have in the back after we drop Mrs. Jefferson off," he interrupted. "That car could hold a lot of shopping bags ..."

He let that thought dangle for a beat or two as my silence spoke volumes. He knew he had me.

"So ... are you game?"

"I'll go," I said.

And so we did. All three of us. And apart from the pit stop we made on the way up to get gas and some Cokes — where the cashier took one look at the hearse and fled to the back of the store with the other frightened employees, begging me to "please just put your money on the counter" — it was a wonderful trip, filled with fabulous dinners, rekindled romance, and plenty of shopping.

To his credit, the valet at the Ritz did his job flawlessly. He got a nice tip that day, and an even better story to tell his wife that night.

SAVED

I need two arrangements," I said, carefully setting the heavy brass containers down on the florist's counter. "The family wants all white — maybe some of those Virginia roses and the Stargazer lilies and a few of your hydrangeas, if you think they'll hold up. The snapdragons too — they look good. No gladiolas, though; Mrs. Dodson never did care for — "

"Dee," the florist interrupted, grabbing both of my hands, "is Johnnie saved?"

I guess I'd known Mr. Wayne Jones for most of my life, and he'd never asked a question like that. He'd done the flowers for H.D. Oliver for as long as I could remember, but usually our conversations centered on casket palls (the big flower arrangement on top of a casket), altar guilds, and the relative merits of a particular rose or lily amid the preponderance of flowers that filled his shop with such a heady perfume.

"Well, I guess so," I said, less convincingly than I intended.

"No, I really want to know. Has he accepted Jesus into

his heart?" Clearly, Wayne Jones was concerned about my husband's spiritual condition. I, however, was on my way to Florida for a tennis trip with my girlfriends, and the only thing standing between me and my plane was the need to get two big, white arrangements on the altar so that Mrs. Dodson, if not her family (who would get a bill that reflected her discerning taste in flowers), could rest in peace.

"Wayne," I said, fluttering my eyelashes a little, "I think Johnnie has done that. But what I really need is for you to do these flowers and deliver them to the church, please."

My attempt at charm was lost on Wayne Jones. He kept gnawing the bone. "Will you ask him? I have to know. Will you make sure? I don't want to get to heaven and find out that John Oliver won't be joining me there. Please?"

"Okay." I laughed. "I will let you know."

I tried to pull my hand away, but Wayne Jones was not letting go — not just yet. "You need to make sure, okay?"

Later that night, I lay in bed next to Johnnie, recapping the day's events like we usually did and making plans for my upcoming trip. Johnnie was going to take some time off to be with the girls, since the sitter I had hired canceled at the last minute.

"Are you saved?"

My question caught Johnnie off guard. "What?" he asked.

"Are you saved?" I repeated. "I was with Mr. Wayne Jones at the shop today, and he was having a complete hissy fit, wanting to make sure you had accepted Jesus into your heart so you would be in heaven with him."

"Yes," Johnnie answered, "I have done that."

"Really? Have you really done it? Because Wayne" — and by this time I was more concerned about Johnnie's salvation than with using Wayne Jones's full and proper name, like we usually did — "is really worried, and I promised him I would make sure. Besides, you are Catholic, and I am not sure if that counts, so just do it again."

Johnnie grew quiet. After a moment, I thought he might have fallen asleep, so I spoke up again. "Well, did you say it? Did you ask Jesus to come into your heart?"

"Yes."

"Do it again," I insisted, as though Wayne Jones was right there with us, hovering over our bed. "I don't trust you. Say it out loud."

"Oh my gosh, Dee!" Johnnie yelled, sitting up and turning toward me. "I have done it!"

"Well, okay then. Good night."

I left for Florida the next morning. It seemed that, overnight, almost everyone in Tidewater had died, so Johnnie could not take any time off. Instead, he took the girls to work. That was nothing new; they'd grown up playing hide-and-seek among the caskets, skipping rope with the velvet pew cords, and using the altar (which featured a state-of-the-art sound system) to stage musicals and dance routines. Where the average person saw headstones in a cemetery, my horse-loving daughters saw an equestrian's dream, transforming the markers into an imaginary steeplechase course. They loved hanging out at the funeral home, and with Johnnie's good-natured boys on hand to watch them ride their tricycles through the garage or climb into the limousines, they never got into much trouble.

(Well, almost never. There was that time when I stopped by after a soccer game with Madison and some of her seven-year-old teammates. They'd all gotten Cokes out of Johnnie's machine — which was okay — and then migrated to the visitation room — which wasn't. We located them just as Madison was making her pitch: if they gave her some money, they could touch the dead person. Ugh. I was aghast, certain that Johnnie and I would be booted out of the Supper Club when word got out. Johnnie, though, just stood there grinning, like maybe he was proud of Madison's entrepreneurial spirit the way other parents admire their kids' lemonade stands. "Aww, Dee Dee," he had said with a wink. "It'll be okay. This kind of stuff isn't socially inappropriate; it's just good old family tradition.")

And so it was that I went to Florida with my girlfriends while Johnnie stayed home and campaigned for Father of the Year. He grilled hot dogs for breakfast, offered the girls candy and chips as side dishes, and let them wash it all down with cans of his favorite drink, Pepsi. After work, they went to Target and Toys "R" Us and bought a bunch of stuff we didn't need, including a new TV for our kitchen. When they picked me up at the airport a few days later, all un-showered and happily hungover from several days of too much candy and too little sleep, we went to Johnnie's favorite restaurant, the Imperial Palace, where the girls regaled me with tales of all the fun they had had. I wanted to reprimand Johnnie for his shoddy parenting, but I couldn't. I had never seen the girls so relaxed and happy. (And dirty, but I wasn't going to let the specter of head lice or tooth decay spoil my homecoming.)

The next day, the painters came to finalize all of the details for the work Johnnie had contracted with them to do on the house. Living in a beach town, we were used to things like pressure washing, painting, and replacing rotting wood, and our home — which we'd been living in for more than ten years — was due for some preventive maintenance. Later that evening, Johnnie went over to my parents' house to put out their trash cans and enjoy a quick visit with them. He came home and climbed into bed.

"Are you in the mood to fool around?" he asked.

"No," I said, "I'm tired." All that playing tennis and shopping and enjoying umbrella drinks with my girlfriends had, I guess, taken its toll. But as I looked over at Johnnie's back and thought about what a great father he was to our girls and what a great son-in-law he was to my parents and what a great provider he was for me (most wives I know have to call their own painters; how lucky was I that my husband actually appreciated the value of good decorating?), I felt myself warming to him.

"Oh, why not?" I said.

We made love slowly and tenderly. Afterward, he said, "I think you are great. I love you."

Those were the last words he ever spoke to me.

Moments later, Johnnie suddenly cried out, "Oh my God! Help me!" He was clutching his head, and I realized, as his speech became garbled, that he was having some sort of a stroke. I dialed 911, and then, my fingers fumbling, I found Johnnie's cell phone and called the first number in his contact list — the office, where one of the boys was always on call. *Come on, come on.* I threw on some clothes and ran downstairs to open the front door. I took the steps three at a time on the way back up, closing the doors to the girls' rooms as I raced back down the hall. Johnnie hadn't moved. I looked at him lying there, so handsome and tan, with his blond hair falling in his face, and my heart leapt into my throat, just like it did the very first time I saw him. He reached over and grabbed my arm and tried to speak, but his words came out all scrambled. Just then, the left side of his face turned down.

"Please, God," I cried, *"stop this — please!"*

I heard footsteps on the stairs, and almost before I knew what was happening, our home was a swirl of red lights and sirens and people moving in and out. Miraculously, the dogs never barked, and mercifully, the girls slept through it all. As the men from the rescue squad put Johnnie into the back of the ambulance, I realized our lives would never be the same. The quiet dream of our love had become a roaring nightmare.

"Don't Let Me Throw Dirt on You!"

he next two days were a blur. One moment, it seemed,
Johnnie and I had been making love; the next, I found
myself fielding a barrage of questions from doctors
and nurses, most of which I had no idea how to answer. They
were trying to stabilize the bleeding in Johnnie's head long
enough so he could be airlifted to the University of Virginia
Medical Center in Charlottesville, but that didn't seem to be
working. I desperately wanted Johnnie to tell me what to do.

"You'd better get it together, John Oliver," I said, looking
into his lovely big brown eyes as he lay, immobile, on the hospital bed. "Don't let me throw dirt on you!"

It was a phrase Johnnie had used whenever I shared my
fear (which was ever-present) that he would die before I did.
He figured there was a fifty-fifty chance I would go first, but
with my grandmother still kicking at the ripe old age of 103,
I knew I had the genetic edge. To even the odds, I'd gotten
Johnnie a gym membership and signed him up to work out

with a personal trainer three times a week. The boys at the office thought it was all one big joke. They'd known Johnnie longer than I had. And sure enough, if I happened to stop in at the office early in the day, more often than not I would find him sitting at his desk, reading the newspaper and eating a Hardee's biscuit, his gym clothes as fresh as they were when he'd left the house an hour or two earlier.

Undeterred, I had resolved to try harder. I fixed dinners that consisted of lean meats and lots of steamed vegetables. I sent Johnnie to work with homemade lunches that featured salads and grilled chicken, along with raw vegetables he could snack on during the day. I thought it was an inspired plan — until the day I popped into the funeral home at lunchtime and found Johnnie and the boys up to their elbows in a bucket of Pollard's fried chicken. A quick scan of the room revealed my lovingly prepared healthy lunch food resting in the trash can. Seeing the steam begin to come out of my ears, the boys grabbed some chicken and bolted from the room, while Johnnie — his chin fairly dripping with grease — looked up and said, "What?"

"For Pete's sake, John!" I had yelled. "I am trying to save you from dying — and you won't even try!"

He had smiled, taken another bite out of the breast he was holding, and said, "Don't let me throw dirt on you!"

Now it looked as if he might get his wish. I was praying he wouldn't die — everyone we knew was praying, from our friends at church to the medical staff at the hospital — but Johnnie's condition seemed to be worsening by the moment.

"Mrs. Oliver?" I heard the doctor behind me, and I stepped outside the room to talk with him. "Here is the latest scan of Johnnie's brain," he said. "The last bleed was huge. I'm afraid there is nothing anyone can do at this point."

I turned and stepped back into Johnnie's room, moving to his bed. His eyes were closed. "Can you hear me, Johnnie?" I asked. "I love you. What do you want me to do?"

Johnnie didn't answer. He just lay there. I wasn't even sure if he had heard me.

I asked someone to get the girls. When they came into the room, I was struck by how little they seemed. I had thought they were bigger, but standing among all of the tubes and monitors, they looked very small and vulnerable.

"Let's hold hands," I instructed. "Let's make a circle around Daddy and say a family prayer."

"God," I began, "we want to thank you for all the days and years we have had together as a family. Bless each and every one of us." I took a breath and felt Jacquie, our eldest, squeeze my hand. "You know the days we have before us. Guide us through them. Hold us tightly and keep us close to you."

Johnnie looked so peaceful. "Girls," I said, "I want you to kiss your daddy and tell him how much you love him." They each did so, in turn.

I felt a strange sense of calm settle over the room. "John," I said firmly, "I want you to know we will be fine. Don't worry about us, okay? Just go on to where you should be, and know that we will never stop loving you."

With that, I began shooing the girls out of the room. "I

am not sure what is going to happen, but no matter what, we will all be fine. Don't forget that." I looked at each one of them. "Do you understand me?" Three little heads all nodded, together.

After they had left, I stood in the room, alone with the man I loved more than life itself. "Oh, Johnnie," I whispered, feeling my strength begin to give way. "You are the best thing that ever happened to me. I have loved growing up with you, and I love you more than you will ever know."

I leaned over and gently kissed his lips. In that moment, I knew he was gone.

The boys came into the room and stood around me, their dark suits forming a protective wall. I looked into their eyes and saw that they'd been crying. My eyes welled up too, and we stood together, silently weeping over the man we all adored.

I don't know whether we stood there for five minutes or an hour; time seemed to stand still. Finally, summoning the courage to voice the words I didn't want to speak, I looked at the boys and broke the silence.

"Take him home."

RITES OF
A SOUTHERN PASSING

*N*ot long ago, a friend showed me a verse she'd found in *The Message*, which is one of our favorite Bibles. Despite my years of parochial schooling, I never did get too comfortable with words like *thee* and *thou*, and I like how straightforward, even sometimes blunt, *The Message* is.

"Crying is better than laughing," it tells us in Ecclesiastes 7:3. "It blotches the face but it scours the heart."

Now, I am not sure crying is necessarily better, but I can certainly vouch for the fact that it blotches the face. When I got home from the hospital that day after Johnnie died, I was a mess. There were cars in the driveway — I saw my friend Denice's, along with a handful of others, both familiar and not — and people carrying food and flowers into the house. I didn't think I could face anyone.

I walked around to the side of the house and sat down in the driveway, burying my face in my hands and sobbing as if my whole world had ended. It felt like it had. I wasn't even sure I could breathe. Why hadn't I been the first one to go?

Suddenly, a hand touched my shoulder. I looked up and saw Carol, the woman who came each Wednesday to help with the laundry. Johnnie always wanted everything to be ironed (including his boxer shorts), and between his high standards and the never-ending flow of dirty clothes from three very active little girls, I needed help. Carol was a godsend.

I looked up at her, and through my tears I delivered the news: Mr. Oliver had died that morning.

"Oh!" Carol gasped, covering her mouth with one hand while the other one reached for her wig, which had slipped sideways on her head. "I am so sorry, Mrs. Oliver."

I'm so sorry. Those were the words Johnnie always said whenever anyone died. Now, coming from this woman with tears in her eyes and her hair on backward, they took on an almost surreal quality.

"I know, Carol," I said, hoisting myself off the concrete. "Thank you."

I made my way into the kitchen, where the rites of a Southern passing were moving forward, full throttle. Lists were being made, food delivered, and the good tablecloths spread out. My friend Leslie had already organized all of my Tupperware. Someone put a chicken salad sandwich in my hand, and I went upstairs, thankful for the army of women who seemed to have everything under control.

I climbed onto the bed with my sandwich and took a bite. Staring at nothing, my mind wandered to the funeral home, where a nameless, faceless woman sat, tall and straight, in the front pew of our chapel. Sometimes she was heavy; sometimes she was thin. Sometimes she looked old; sometimes far less so. Sometimes she wore the fancy clothes of a well-heeled world traveler; sometimes she looked simple and plain, as if maybe she had never left the city limits. Always, though, she sat there … and more often than not, her shoulders eventually drooped. She was the widow in the front row, and watching her grief, year in and year out, I knew one thing: I cared for her, even if I didn't know her, but I never, ever wanted to be her.

And now I was.

I heard footsteps in the hallway, and with a start, my mind jerked back to reality. Someone protested that I was not to be disturbed, but the door burst open anyway. Madison bounded into the room and announced, "Momma, the boys are here!"

"I can see that," I said, looking past Madison to the crowd of men whose frames now filled my bedroom doorway. "What's up, guys?"

"We're here to get something," one of them offered.

"Here to get what?" I asked.

"Well," Sam began — and right away I could tell I might not get the full story. Sam was Johnnie's ever-present sidekick and closest confidant, and I was sure he knew things about my husband that I never would. Looking at him now, his strawberry blond hair cropped close to his head, I realized he had to be feeling Johnnie's loss every bit as keenly as I did. They had been like brothers — Johnnie the well-dressed, mild-mannered diplomat, and Sam the tobacco-chewing, tattooed redneck who was as proud of his vintage pickup truck as he was of his big, shiny Hummer, his collection of motorcycles, and his gun. Two very different men on the outside, the same good-hearted soul underneath. And since Sam worked as a bail bondsman on the side, tooling around town in an old station wagon, he was never without a side-splitting story about his suburban-style bounty hunting. We were never quite sure how much of it was true and how much he made up, but his tales kept us laughing.

But no one was laughing now.

Numbly, I realized Sam was still speaking. "John said that if he ever died, we had to get over here real quick and get something out of the house."

With that, the boys turned on their heels and made their way to the attic stairs. Madison and I followed close behind. My head cleared the landing just as Sam was pulling back some of the insulation that ran between the rafters.

"What on earth are you looking for?" I demanded.

They didn't answer, focusing on pulling back more of the puffy pink sheets. "I thought he said it would be here," one of them muttered.

I couldn't begin to imagine what secrets my husband had hidden in the deepest recesses of our home. Body parts? Surely he would have cremated those. Drugs or booze? That hardly seemed likely; I could barely get him to take an aspirin, and Johnnie, relishing his role as a father to our growing girls, had given up drinking anything harder than a Pepsi.

The boys continued their search, but I was too exhausted

to care. I went back to my bedroom to await the news about whatever they discovered. I could hear them tromping around, covering what must have been every last inch of storage space. Finally, they lumbered back down the steps.

"We couldn't find what he told us to get."

"Maybe it would help," I said, sighing, "if you told me what you are supposed to be looking for."

The boys exchanged a look. "Okay," Sam said. "Guns."

"Guns! Guns? Like, how many guns?"

"Well . . ." Here again, I had the distinct sense that Sam was holding out on me. "A few guns."

I knew Johnnie had a gun; he'd used it one summer morning to shoot at the ducks that had taken to swimming (and doing other, more offensive things) in our pool. I'd been lounging in bed when I heard the first few bangs. I rushed outside to behold Johnnie, the mighty hunter — buck naked on our balcony, taking aim at the trespassers. I intervened in time to save the birds (and, hopefully, Johnnie's good name among the neighbors), but not, alas, the pool liner. It was a goner.

Johnnie knew I thought guns were dangerous, and that I didn't want them anywhere near our girls. It was no wonder, I realized, that he had hidden his stash from me. Particularly if he had more than one weapon.

"Guns?" Madison said, peeking into the room. "I know where they are!"

We all turned and watched, speechless, as Madison crossed the bedroom and flung open the door to our closet. Falling to her knees, she shoved aside several pairs of Johnnie's pants and reached her little hand back into the darkness. "Here's one of them!" she cried, tugging a giant case and scattering Johnnie's shoes. "And ... another!"

I could tell, just looking at the cases, that Johnnie definitely had more than two guns. "And don't forget the bullets!" Madison cried, brandishing a large box and handing it to Sam.

"Good grief!" I said, as the boys unpacked the cases and spread the arsenal out across my white duvet cover. "Are there any more secrets I don't know about?"

They shook their heads.

"Madison," I prompted, "does Daddy have anything else hidden in the house?"

"Nope," she said. "I think that's it."

The boys left, taking the guns, as well as the suit Johnnie would have wanted to be buried in. I decided to take a shower. Maybe my tears wouldn't seem so darn wet if I mixed them under fifty gallons of hot water.

A couple of hours later, Sam called. "Johnnie is ready," he said. "I am going to come and pick you up."

The boys met me at the door to the funeral home, and together we walked down the hall to our largest viewing room. I'd walked that hallway a million times; never before had it seemed so long.

"Remember how you always used to worry about Johnnie dying?" Sam asked.

"Yes," I replied, "I remember that."

"Well," he said, "you don't have to worry about that anymore!"

I stopped in my tracks. "What did you just say?" I asked, incredulous.

"Only that you don't have to worry about Johnnie dying anymore."

With that, one of the other boys punched Sam in the shoulder, sending him hurtling into the wall. It was okay. I had been surprised by Sam's tactlessness, but not offended; I knew he meant well.

And in a weird way, Sam was right. My worst fear in all the world had come to pass, and I was still standing there, breathing. I would survive — some way, somehow.

But I knew what had to happen first.

I would have to become the widow in the front pew. It was not a position I wanted to assume, and I wasn't at all sure I could do it. I knew I had sounded strong and confident when I had told Johnnie not to worry about us, but I had no idea what the future would hold for me or for my girls.

I breathed a silent prayer: *God, you are going to have to stick close. I cannot do this on my own.* And I continued down the hall to do what had to be done.

I had seen hundreds of bodies over the years. It didn't matter who they had been in life — rich or poor, young or old, good-looking or common — they all seemed sort of, well, *tidy* in death. Tucked in. Peaceful, regardless of the stresses life may have served up to them. I know that's partly due to the embalming process — and Sam, to his credit, was among the most skilled professionals I had ever known, sometimes getting people to look even better in death than in life. (And had he been a plastic surgeon instead of a funeral director, my mother would surely have discovered his talents.) Even so, I was not prepared for how beautiful Johnnie would appear. Sam led me to the viewing room and then stepped away, giving me one last moment alone with Johnnie. I wanted to make time stand still.

But I couldn't, of course. It seemed, in fact, to speed up, and before I knew it, we were on our way to Galilee. Nearly two thousand people crammed into every nook and cranny of the church, lining the walls and filling the balcony, with others standing in the halls and overflow rooms. The girls and I sat in the front row and held each other's hands. They wore new dresses that, I learned, had been purchased by Leslie — God bless that woman.

Of course, the girls had peppered me with all sorts of questions: Why had this happened? Had Daddy been sick? Was God punishing us for something?

I didn't have the answers, at least not all of them. But I could tell my daughters this: God was not punishing us. He had blessed our family, and he was not going to stop. He would take care of us. He would, as he promised in the Bible, meet all our needs, from giving the girls lasting memories of their dad grilling hot dogs for breakfast, to giving me a freshly painted house before I would have even noticed the decay, to letting us know — thanks to Mr. Wayne Jones and his unrelenting questions — that we could absolutely, positively, look forward to seeing their precious daddy in heaven.

PART
TWO

They Say
It Gets Easier

"I Am So Sorry for Your Loss"

I am so sorry for your loss."

If I heard Johnnie say those words once, I probably heard him say them a thousand times. I would tease him — we all would — and challenge him to come up with something more original or creative as he met with grieving families or spoke with people at funerals and receptions. But he never wavered. He'd just stand there, looking handsome in his black suit, shaking hands with people and telling them how sorry he was.

The thing is, he really meant it. Johnnie knew the pain of losing someone you love, and he was smart enough to realize that nothing he could say — no word of wisdom or sage bit of advice — would "fix it." He'd always offer to help and ask if there was anything a family needed, but mostly, he just understood.

I am so sorry. In the days and weeks that followed Johnnie's death, those four little words came to mean more than I could ever have imagined they would. Stacked against the reams of well-meaning condolences (and unsolicited advice) that I got from family members, friends, and neighbors, and even an old boyfriend (who thought it would help if I treated myself to a new flat-screen TV), the simple sentiment of being just plain *sorry* became the most powerful offering anyone could give.

Back when Sam tried to comfort me with the "blessing" of my no longer having to worry about Johnnie's death, I figured nothing could top that one in the "well-intentioned but utterly unhelpful" condolences category. I was wrong. Even the old standby — "He's in a better place" — began to sting a bit. Did everyone really think Johnnie's life with me had been all that bad?

Maybe it was to be expected, given the lack of economic diversity in our social circles, but I began to lose count of how many people were concerned not just with my emotional well-being but with whether or not I'd be able to keep up with the country club dues:

Will your husband's company survive?

Do you have enough money?

Will you have to get another job? Sell your house?

Call us if you want to sell your house.

Then, too, there were the "experts" who analyzed our new family dynamic and offered all manner of meant-to-be-positive observations:

I bet it is nice not to have to hear Johnnie snore anymore.

It is good that the girls are so young.

It is good that the girls are so old.

Do you think this will affect the girls?

It is better to be widowed than divorced.

Now you don't have to argue over anything; you get to make all the decisions yourself!

If such unflaggingly upbeat comments made me squirm, they were nothing compared to the barrage of concerns and what-ifs I heard almost daily from friends who probably meant their questions and advice to sound practical. In many cases, though, the effect was actually kind of depressing:

Are you going to sell or give away Johnnie's clothes? His lawn mower?

Are you scared to sleep alone in that house? Are you afraid someone will break in?

I don't know how you are able to go to events and functions all by yourself. I could never do that!

I bet it is hard to go to church after you had his funeral there.

Are you worried about being alone forever?

I hadn't, actually, started to worry about the future. I wasn't too scared to be home alone; I had saved one of Johnnie's guns, and I knew how to use it. And given Johnnie's unpredictable work hours, I had been forced to attend social gatherings alone in the past, and I didn't think that becoming a widow would also mean becoming a hermit. But as the days and weeks wore on, I began to grow a little bit concerned about where my life might be headed — particularly since the running commentary from almost everyone who knew me showed no sign of letting up:

You must be overwhelmed.

You look tired.

You should seek counseling.

Of course I needed counseling! How else could I be expected to process Johnnie's death — and still have any energy left to cope with the people who kept trying to comfort me? I've read his story, and believe me, Job didn't hear the half of it. At least *his* friends didn't have access to match.com! Everyone, it seemed, wanted to see me get back in the saddle:

Do you think you will marry again?

I know someone you should date.

You should get married again — right away!

It is good that you are so young. You look good; you can get married again.

The grass hadn't even started growing on Johnnie's grave before friends and neighbors started trying to fix me up. After a while, even my daughters began hinting around that I might want to start husband hunting in earnest. It was as though, knowing I'd spent time in a Catholic school, they thought I might seriously consider becoming a nun. Or maybe they were just worried I would put on an old, holey sweater and start collecting stray cats. I don't know. But as the weeks turned into months and I didn't show much interest in dating, the conversations started to get a bit weird. Maybe folks assumed that once death was already on the table, nothing was off-limits. Even casual acquaintances — people I'd run into in the grocery store — began to sound eerily like Dr. Ruth:

Have you thought about having sex with someone else?

Are you worried about having sex with someone else?
Maybe you should have sex.

I wasn't sure how to answer questions or suggestions like these, so I didn't. I hoped the look on my face might be enough to direct the conversation back to a more pleasant topic, like the weather. Or Syrian refugees. Anything. Some people, though, just couldn't take a hint, and I found myself longing to run into someone who would just look at me and say, "It's okay. Everything will be all right."

I know that, except for a few rubberneckers, most people were genuinely concerned about me and about our girls. Looking back, I suspect that many people are just plain uncomfortable when it comes to death, and they blurt out things without really thinking about what they are saying. Maybe it's an unwillingness to confront their own mortality. Or maybe they think people who work in the funeral business must be somehow immune to the pain of saying good-bye, since we are surrounded by grief all the time.

My favorite (well, actually, my least favorite) question from the peanut gallery was one I heard several times but never managed to answer: *How long do you think it will take you to get over Johnnie's death?*

How long does it take to get over the loss of someone you love? I don't know. I don't think you ever really do.

But life does go on, and as the weeks and months went by, I found the answers forming more easily on my tongue:

I am not in a hurry to sell our home, but if I do, you will see a sign in the yard.

Yes, the bed is empty, but some combination of two dogs and three girls usually fill it on any given night.

Will I marry again? Someone has to ask first, and then I can decide.

I was raised that it is bad manners to talk about money, politics, or sex.

Everything will work itself out.

Everything will work itself out. That was a truth I clung to, one that I desperately wanted to believe. And I did believe it, particularly when I was surrounded by friends who came bearing chicken salad and ham biscuits — the Smithfield kind, not the ones made with some lame deli ham. Those definitely helped.

So what *do* you say to someone who has lost a loved one? At the risk of sounding unoriginal, I must defer to Johnnie, the man who got it right. Just say, "I am so sorry for your loss. What can I do to help?"

And then listen.

Pink Jobs, Blue Jobs

*L*ike most couples, I guess, Johnnie and I had our ups and downs, our quarrels and our reconciliations, our shared likes and our individual pet peeves. Ours was not the perfect union, but we did have good communication, good sex, and a good plan for keeping our household (and our marriage) running smoothly: pink jobs were for me; blue jobs were his.

I took the kids to the doctor, ran the vacuum cleaner, picked up the dry cleaning, and shopped for groceries. Johnnie mowed the lawn (meticulously), took the cars to the shop when it was time to rotate the tires (he was never late), replaced the furnace (that is to say, he picked out a new one when ours blew up and then hired someone to install it), and paid the bills.

Sometimes I think this blue-pink divide (which is probably more common than the gender-blender crowd might want to admit) is why most widowers don't stay single as long as their female counterparts do. You can put off an oil change for weeks — months even. And the utility companies send "past due" notices before you find yourself without gas or water. (Trust me.) But coffee? You gotta have that, and if making it is a pink job (as it was in our house) and the guy can't even figure out where his dear, departed wife kept the filters, he's a sitting duck. The ladies — particularly if he is a churchgoer — will show up, casseroles in hand, and start perking more than the coffee.

(If you're a guy and you're reading this, and you are offended that I don't think you could make yourself a cup of coffee, let me just ask you one thing: Do you read directions? I thought not. That's okay; Johnnie never did either. When he got a new gadget or toy, he'd skip the owner's manual and just "figure it out." And I had to hand it to him. He always found a way to make things work. When he got his first cell phone, for instance, he thought having the walkie-talkie kind would be pretty cool — must be a guy thing — and he got them for all of the boys. We'd be standing at some poor soul's graveside, and the GI Joe contraption would go off: *Johnnie? Hey, Johnnie, can you hear me?* Of course he could hear — and so could all of the grieving family members and anyone within about a mile of the cemetery. Not having read the instructions, Johnnie would have no idea how to mute the doggone thing, so he'd step back from the group, cock his arm, and hurl the phone into the field of headstones, like it was some sort of grenade. Afterward, he'd recruit the girls and me to go find it, like we were hunting for Easter eggs. It wasn't a method endorsed by the manufacturer, but it worked.)

Women, I am convinced, generally last longer. But that's not to say we find it easy. The early months of my widowhood felt like a crash course in home maintenance: Whom should I call to fix the leaky roof? What about the rotten window Johnnie never got around to replacing? Does the mulch automatically show up in the garden twice a year, or do I have to call somebody? And how, exactly, does one go about starting a lawn mower?

And the bills! Who knew they came so often? Sure, I checked the mail — for things like catalogs and party invitations. But all of that other junk — the power bill, the city utilities, the credit card statements — eek! Johnnie's name was on those envelopes; I had never once considered reading "his" mail.

Now, though, those letters belonged to me. I knew I had to change the name on the accounts, which meant I needed about eight copies of Johnnie's death certificate to give to our creditors. The power company and the utility people made the swap, no questions asked. Nordstrom was equally willing to help; they were so accommodating, in fact, that I half expected them to send flowers along with my new credit card.

The phone company, however, was another story. I think they had a harder time coming to grips with Johnnie's passing than I did. "I am so sorry for your loss," they would say whenever I tried to explain the situation, "but we cannot discuss the details of this account with anyone other than the account holder. May we speak to Mr. Oliver, please?" Finally I just gave up. Call me an enabler, but if the phone company couldn't let go of Johnnie, I wasn't going to force them. Now whenever the repairman comes to the house to fix a problem with one of our phones, I simply pretend that my husband is "unavailable." Which, I guess, he is.

I jumped through similar hoops with our insurance carrier, our home security provider, and our mortgage company, none of which seemed willing to believe Johnnie was dead. No one wanted that to be untrue more than I did, but facts were facts — and I needed to be able to pay the bills. I needed to do the blue jobs.

Looking back, it would have been smart if we'd put the bills in *both* of our names. Ditto for bank accounts, investments, car titles, and safe deposit boxes. Maybe husbands and wives ought to give each other a short course on the basics of what they each do, or make a list of important contacts, like the vet or the name of your child's second-grade teacher. Failing that, we should at least do what one of my girlfriends did when it dawned on her that her husband had never fixed himself a meal in their twenty-eight years of marriage. Not wanting him to starve to death if she met an untimely demise, she gave him the thumbs-up to scope out the crowd at her funeral for her replacement.

But no amount of scoping or list making or proper naming can prepare you for *every* eventuality. There will always be blue jobs and pink jobs you didn't see coming.

Like when you wake up one day and find a snake in your kitchen.

I did what any woman would do in a life-threatening emergency; I called 911. Turns out, the rescue squad doesn't handle snakes, at least not until they bite. Instead, they gave me the name of a good exterminator — a nice gesture, but I was not exactly willing to fix a cup of coffee and keep an eye on my unwelcome guest until they arrived. Instead, I did the next logical thing: I ran outside.

Thanks be to God, there was a man — a real Man, from the neighbor's lawn service — outside. "Help me! Help me!" I cried, wielding the shovel I'd grabbed from the garage on my way out.

To his credit, the fellow did not jump in his truck and drive off (as I would have done if I had seen a crazy woman with a shovel coming at me like a linebacker). Instead, he assessed the situation, grabbed his hoe, and made short work of my problem.

I love men. And had the lawn guy not been wearing a wedding ring, I might have invited him to stay for coffee.

A Hearse Pulling
a U-Haul

*M*aybe it's a good thing there is so much to do in the days and weeks that come after a funeral. Whether you are changing the name on the power bill or killing a snake in the kitchen, it is nice to stay busy — but not just for the reason you might suspect. Oh, sure, the daily to-do lists and constant flow of friends and neighbors definitely help keep grief at bay (for a few minutes, anyway), but the post-funeral hubbub had the added advantage of serving as a legitimate (and, in my case, welcome) distraction from other pressing matters. Like, literally pressing. As in, pressing against the door of the closet that I could barely shut because of all the stuff in there.

I will let you in on a little secret. I am a connoisseur of reality television (I still marvel over that woman who sewed little outfits for squirrels in *My Strange Obsession*), and one of my favorite programs is *Hoarders*. I watch the show because it makes me feel like an organized person. This is an illusion, of course, but I like to pretend. In reality, I am a "level 1 hoarder." The kind of person whose home looks, to a casual observer, to be neat and tidy. And on the surface, it is. Just don't open my closets.

Or, for that matter, my drawers. Or the attic. Or anywhere you could put almost anything, because chances are, I have. If you were to ask me where you might find, say, a spare lightbulb, I will have a general idea of which domestic quadrant it is in, but to actually get to it, I will have to open any number of cabinets in the kitchen and the laundry room before moving on to search in the garage, where I will undoubtedly find the flower bucket I haven't seen since last April or the wrapping paper I meant to put away with the Christmas decorations. Ultimately, I will forget what it was I went out there to find.

I save things. Sometimes I do it for sentimental reasons, like the ugly wool plaid skirt that was part of my high school uniform. Sometimes I hang on to something because I am sure my children will one day want it (I might not use that cracked chip-and-dip platter, but it would be good for a college apartment, right?). And sometimes, I save things just because I can — and because I have this strange but recurring nightmare that I will one day be a homeless person and will want to have some stuff to push around in my cart.

Johnnie, of course, was just the opposite. He despised clutter. If we hadn't used something in a few months, his mantra was, "We don't need it; give it away, or toss it." He regarded my hodgepodge collection of attic treasures and my overstuffed closets in much the same way a man might look at a woman after he has been away at sea for a few months. Johnnie would come down the hall, a big, black trash bag in hand, and he'd be practically drooling. "Please!" I would say, the panic rising in my chest. "Let's set aside a day when we can tackle this project together. It will be more fun that way, I promise!"

Sometimes I would fool him. More often, though, he'd simply smile, edge past me, and start sorting.

When he died, it took me about forty-eight hours to realize my plight. A level 1 hoarder without her Mr. Clean is just asking for trouble, and I knew it. Johnnie hadn't been out of the house for even a week, and already things were finding their way into strange places. I opened the pantry and found my curlers. What the—? Oh, yeah. I was in a hurry that morning. No time to run back upstairs.

Thankfully, God knew my secret sins even better than I did (isn't there a Bible verse about that?), and he sent reinforcements. My friend Leslie, as I think I mentioned earlier, organized my Tupperware. She also went through our home office and got all the papers in order. And then, after the initial rush of chicken casseroles and ham biscuits subsided, she even cleaned out my refrigerator. But I wasn't about to subject her—or anyone else—to the deepest recesses of my linen closet or the murky darkness under my bed. Last I checked, there was part of a seventh-grade science project (unfinished) under there.

I eyed the children. I wasn't sure how much longer I had to live—forty-five years, tops—and I wondered how bad it would be, really, if I just left all the junk for my girls to handle one day. After all Johnnie and I had done for them (he got a reverse vasectomy, for goodness' sake!), I figured they owed us.

They probably did, but I couldn't saddle them with the job either. It was just too ... awful. And I knew that, left untreated, the clutter would only grow, like a cancer.

I had no choice. I started cleaning. And sorting. And giving stuff away. And, yes, even tossing it. I was sure that, from his perch in the clouds, Johnnie was drinking a Pepsi, watching me — and beaming. I can hear him now: "See, Dee? You're never gonna see a hearse pulling a U-Haul. You really can't take it with you."

Maybe not. But they might just have to bury me in my old plaid skirt. I haven't been able to bring myself to part with that. I guess I figure that if I made it through all those years of Catholic school, I'm going to want to show up in heaven looking like I earned it.

HENRY AND THE
NO-CHANGE RULE

*N*o change for a year."

That's the mantra of all grief counselors, particularly those who work in the funeral business. When you lose a loved one, don't make any sudden moves. No new jobs. No new house. No new haircut. Just keep steady.

That makes sense, really. We take comfort in the familiar — old slippers, old chairs, old books, old friends. And I think that, when someone dies, God activates some sort of divine bubble wrap. It's like a protective, shock-absorbing system for your emotions, and it's designed to shield you from the outside world and give you time to process your grief. Wrapped in this buffer (which lasts for about a year), you can adjust to your new reality at a deliberate, unhurried pace. If you try to speed up the process, you will likely find yourself having to backtrack later — and believe me, you don't want to crisscross through the tangled Forest of Adjustment any more times than you have to.

Some of your well-meaning friends and family members might advise you to short-circuit the mourning period and "move on" or "embrace life" in any number of ways. People will encourage you to sell your husband's golf clubs, redecorate your kitchen, get a nose job, or try dating. And while I have nothing against any of these ideas — and, if my mother is to be believed, plastic surgery is almost as good as a ham biscuit when it comes to chasing the blues away — they can wait. Move too soon, and you'll pop the bubble wrap.

Instead, surround yourself with all that is familiar, reassuring, and good. Your whole world has been upended, and you need as much stability as you can find — particularly if you have children, who thrive on the security blanket of "sameness." Of course, there may be financial or other factors that necessitate some degree of change, but don't make the mistake of thinking that just doing something — anything — will make you feel better.

Trust me, I know.

As a funeral director's widow, I figured the "no change" rule did not apply to me. I was no amateur; I'd been walking other people through the grieving process for more than twenty years. And even though I'd kept Johnnie's sunglasses on the bookshelf (right where he'd left them), I had rearranged the living room furniture — and the girls and I were still standing. Plus, I'd survived phase one of the Great Clutter Clean-Out. Sure, Johnnie's suits were still hanging in our closet and his precious lawn mower still took up half the garage, but I'd made a few changes — I upgraded my phone, for instance — and I seemed to have suffered no ill effects. I was feeling strong. How wrong could it be if I tried to "tweak" our lives with a little bit of happiness?

Perhaps a little bit of background is in order. A month or so before Johnnie died, we had made the excruciatingly difficult decision to put our dog — our wonderful, well-trained, perfect dog — to sleep. I considered Spot some of my best work (he was better behaved, by far, than any of our children), and when he got sick, I was devastated. We all were. Spot had been part of our family for eight years.

A few weeks after Johnnie's funeral, I found myself consumed by a seemingly unquenchable sadness, and I began to miss Spot with a renewed vigor. What a comfort he would be to me and the girls! What a source of joy he would provide, were he still around to greet us in the kitchen every morning, to lie at my feet while I read the paper, to snuggle with the girls while they watched *Who's Your Baby's Daddy?* Nothing I could do would bring Spot back, but I thought that perhaps I could re-create the dog.

"Vicki?" I said, calling on my faithful sidekick of a cousin. After all, if she'd picked Johnnie from the litter of available bachelors, surely she could help me find a dog. "I miss Spot."

"I know you do."

"So I called the breeder. She has one — "

"What breeder?" Vicki wanted to know.

"Spot's breeder. A gal named Sally. She's got one standard poodle left from their latest batch, and he's black, just like Spot. Will you come with me?"

Vicki knew the breeder's kennel was four hours away, but I was counting on the fact that almost no one says no to a grieving widow. Sure enough, she agreed to go, and I picked her up the next day.

I should have known something wasn't right when we arrived at the kennel and were greeted by a pair of beasts that looked more suited for saddles than leashes. "Meet Duke and Daisy," Sally said, scratching one of the dogs behind an ear. "They're Henry's parents."

"Who's Henry?" I asked.

"Your dog! Well, that is" — here Sally paused for a second — "if you want him."

I followed Sally around the corner of her house to the kennel out back, the place where we'd adopted our beloved Spot. Duke and Daisy followed at her heels, like well-behaved giants.

"This is Henry!" Sally announced, motioning toward a dog that was, convict-like, trying to stage an escape by digging under his fence. Intent on completing his mission, Henry ignored us.

"Henry!" Sally repeated, louder this time.

Henry kept digging. He was bigger than I'd expected him to be, far less cuddly-looking than Spot had been as a puppy.

"How old is Henry?" I inquired.

"Let's see now," Sally said, not meeting my eye. "I guess he's about four months old."

Four months. That meant that other would-be owners had probably come and gone, eyeballing Henry but passing him by. To his credit, Henry didn't look at all troubled by the rejection; he seemed content to dig.

"Is he — trained?" I wasn't quite sure how to put the question; I hoped Sally would get my drift.

"He's mostly there," Sally replied. "He just needs a good home. Someone to love him."

Looking at Henry, I felt myself softening. Don't get me wrong — there was nothing all that attractive about this pure-bred, half-grown, antisocial mongrel. But even as he turned his back on me and found a new place to dig, I found myself longing to take him home. To train him. To love him into perfection, as I had his ancestor (at least I wanted to think it was his ancestor), Spot. Spot, the magnificent.

"I'll take him."

Vicki and I loaded Henry into the car. As I eased in behind the wheel, I heard a retching sound. Henry, it seemed, had thrown up.

"Some dogs don't like cars," Sally offered. "He'll be all right as soon as you get on the road."

Henry was not, as it turned out, "all right." Not even close. He barfed when we got to the highway, and then again an hour or so down the road. Any woman with half a brain would have turned the car around right then and there, but all I could see was the happy faces of my daughters when they saw — surprise! — what I had done. They had a hole in their hearts; I was going to fill it with a new dog. I would be their savior.

And the girls *were* happy. They were ecstatic, in fact, and I congratulated myself on my success.

The boys at the funeral home weren't so sure. "You just lost *Johnnie*," Sam said — as though, after barely a month, I might have forgotten. "Have you lost your *mind* too? You, of all people, should know about the one-year rule."

Immune to their chastisement, I smugly crossed my arms. "Puppies," I said, "don't count as change."

What's that saying in the Bible? Something about how pride goeth before Dee's fall? Hold on a sec, while I look it up.

Here it is. Proverbs 16:18: "Pride goes before destruction, a haughty spirit before a fall."

Now, I know the good Lord wrote the Bible with everyone in mind, and it's not like any one of us has a corner on his warnings. But when I read that verse — when I saw that word *destruction* — I couldn't help but think that, way back in the beginning, God must have been thinking of me.

Destruction doesn't begin to cover it. Four chewed-up kitchen chairs, one partially devoured wall, and about half of a newly reupholstered sofa later, I had to concede that the boys were right. I backtracked through the Forest of Adjustment and found Henry a new home. He became the beloved pet of a family who, evidently, didn't mind the degree of "change" he supplied.

I, meanwhile, found a good therapist.

Puppies, like nose jobs and new boyfriends, can wait — for at least a year. And maybe even two.

Just
Get Out There

I patched up the wall, replaced a few chairs, and called Johnnie's decorator to see what could be done about the sofa (which was now more of a half-sofa) Henry had polished off. That done, I turned my attention to ... nothing. I had cleaned out the closets (well, as clean as they were ever going to get), written about a zillion thank-you notes, and spent way too much money on pre-lit Christmas trees, hair vitamins, and other "as seen on TV" must-haves during my late-night online shopping sprees. As the months wore on (and the flow of visitors left, taking their Tupperware with them), the truth became increasingly clear: I had no social life.

Professionally, I stayed busy. I continued to help out at the funeral home, and our home phone still rang at all hours with friends and neighbors who had lost loved ones and didn't know where to turn. I never minded those calls; I knew Johnnie would have dropped everything to help anybody who needed him, and I wanted to do the same.

Personally, though, I had settled into a less-than-stimulating routine. I still went to parties, but I never stayed long (and I never forgot my mother's admonition about drinking: "One glass of wine at a party; the bottle at home if you need it"). I forced myself to go out to eat, sometimes taking the girls and sometimes going alone, on the theory that it was good to simply get out of the house at least once each week. And I honed my skills as a sommelier, learning which wines paired best with which cereals on a Friday night when the girls were off with their friends and I cozied up to another episode of *Say Yes to the Dress.*

Thus it was that, with the one-year anniversary of Johnnie's death approaching (and Madison hinting that it was time to call the game on my self-imposed mourning), I began to think about dating.

The whole idea scared me to death.

I hadn't had a date since I was twenty-three years old, which was more years ago than I will ever admit. (In addition to her rules about social drinking, Jacquie Branch had a long list of "don'ts" when it came to aging. "Don't tell anyone how old you are," she'd warn, the way other parents talked to their kids about doing drugs or talking to strangers. "Never. Ever. No matter what." And she didn't. I never knew how old she was. My father never knew. The DMV never knew. When she passed away — which was, unbelievably, just a few months after Johnnie died — my father and I just took our best guess in the obituary and then rounded down, lest she haunt us.)

I wasn't even sure where to begin. I polled my girlfriends,

but it soon became obvious that, having been off the market themselves for a quarter-century or more, they had no idea what the dating scene looked like. I thought about asking my daughters, but (1) they were still in middle school (and, I hoped, still naive about such things), and (2) I didn't really want help from a trio of females whose ideal man came with a bass guitar and a band of brothers, at least half of whom hadn't yet started to shave. Oh, for the days of high school, when all of the eligible bachelors were clumped together under one big roof and your mother could run their names through the grapevine to get the lowdown on all of them. Background checks used to be so simple.

I like to think of myself as a tech-savvy gal (I'd stack my online shopping prowess up against any Neiman's cardholder), so I did the only thing I could think of. I Googled.

What I wanted was an article on dating — as in, how to do it. Where people went. What people wore. Did you meet a guy at a restaurant, or was he supposed to pick you up? Was it better to just have drinks? Lunch, even? Were there certain conversation topics that were taboo these days? Would I be expected to pay?

I found none of that. Instead, what I got was page after page of dating websites, catering to all manner of interests, ages, and sexual preferences. Scrolling through the options — and getting more intrigued and more grossed out, by turns — I finally stumbled upon this bit of free advice:

With tens of millions of singles using online dating services each month, using one of the best dating websites is an easy way to expand your current dating options. If you're looking to get married, you'll want to choose a service with similarly marriage-minded singles. If you prefer casual romances or brief encounters, you may also enjoy sites that cater to singles who prefer more casual encounters. And if you just want to meet someone and see where things go, using the dating sites with the largest possible user base will provide you with the best odds of success.

Brief encounters? Odds of success? Had the world gone to Vegas without me? And what about the other ten million singles out there, all tacking up unrealistically attractive pictures of themselves with captions like, "At home in a T-shirt, but totally comfortable in a tuxedo," or "Willing to fight for my right to party"?

Seriously?

Storage Wars and a glass of cabernet had never looked so good.

I went back to my sofa — and I might have even started sucking my thumb — but then my friend Denice called. Of all my happily married friends, Denice is the one who was most recently swimming in the dating pool, so I guess she knew as much as anyone about what I should expect, or what I should do. Her advice, like Nike's, didn't leave a lot of room for excuses:

"Just do it," Denice said. "Just get out there. It will be easy."

Bolstered by such deep and infinite wisdom, I reluctantly agreed to get back in the proverbial saddle. It wasn't long before someone offered to set me up on a blind date.

My friends thought I was nuts. Who goes on a blind

date when you are fifty-forty-something? But, remembering Johnnie, and the way his hair fell over his eye when I saw him on that blind date all those years ago, I figured it might be my lucky strategy. And after all, it was just for lunch. I said yes.

Four outfits and a zillion insecure thoughts later — why hadn't I taken my mother's advice and seen a plastic surgeon instead of scarfing down all that chicken salad? — I walked into the restaurant and looked around. My date might have been blind, but the other patrons weren't. I immediately recognized at least three people, one of whom had been a good friend of Johnnie's.

Darn. I had driven twelve miles to this restaurant, thinking it would be far enough off the grid.

I had just finished updating Johnnie's friend on the girls' lives (Jacquie had recently decided to find out if blondes really did have more fun, and I hadn't had the heart to say no, since what's a trip to the hair salon when stacked against all of the other teenage possibilities?) when my date walked in. I was sure it was him. He had a bad haircut, a pullover sweater the moths had clearly been storing for him, and at least two inches to go if he wanted to look me in the eye.

But I was hungry.

"Hi," I said, without preamble, "I'm Dee. You must be Steven."

Steven stood there, mute, just looking at me. I couldn't tell if he liked what he saw or if he thought I was an alien.

"Shall we grab a table?" I offered.

"Yes."

We sat down, and right away I could tell it was not, despite Denice's optimism, going to be "easy." As Steven continued to stare, I groped about for an opener. I hated myself as soon as the words came out of my mouth — it felt so unoriginal — but I was truly at a loss for anything even remotely creative: "What do you do for a living?"

"Well," he began, "I am kind of in between jobs right now. I haven't found exactly what I enjoy."

I figured it was up to Steven's father to give him the "work isn't always fun, son" talk, so I skipped to my next question: "What do you like to do in your spare time?"

Ouch. What was I thinking? All of his time was "spare" time. But if Steven took offense, he didn't show it; in fact, it was as if the question popped some sort of cork in his psyche, and he started talking. And talking. And talking. An hour later, I figured I knew all there was to know about the man, and one thing was certain: he didn't need a date; he needed a therapist, a loan officer, a new home, a job, a doctor, and perhaps even an attorney, given the size and scope of his troubles. Lunch was done, and so was I.

I left the restaurant and drove straight home — home, that is, to the funeral home, where I knew I could count on the boys to cheer me up.

"Tell us everything!" they said, crowding around me like a pack of so many hens. "How was it?"

"There is nothing to tell," I said, slumping down into Johnnie's favorite chair. "I would rather date one of the guys back there in the prep room right now than do this ever again."

"Oh, Dee," Sam said, taking me by the hand, "it will be okay. I'll marry you if nobody else comes along."

"I mean," he hedged, "if you don't get too old first."

"Thanks," I said, and closed my eyes. It wasn't the first time Sam had made that offer. He was always going on about how old I was getting — and coming up with ways to help save me from a near-certain spinsterhood in which I would, he suggested, be doomed to watch infomercials and drink wine glasses full of Boost.

Most of the time, I dismissed Sam's overtures for what they were — the ramblings of a gregarious man who felt sure his advice was always welcome, if not always sound. Every once in a while, though, he came up with a scheme that would make my heart stop. Like the time he walked into the office, not too long after Johnnie had died, and announced that he had purchased cemetery property right next to ours.

"You did what?" I had asked. "Where?"

"Cemetery property. I got some. I picked the spot right beside you, Beautiful, so I can be next to you forever. You and Johnnie, that is."

My mouth dropped open and stayed that way — long enough, my mother would have said, for every fly in Tidewater to land in it.

"I am thinking of installing a sprinkler system," Sam said. "And maybe a fence, so other people can't get so close. Would you like that?"

I sat, transfixed, a human flytrap.

"Dee," Sam persisted, "did you hear me? Would you like a

fence? And I got a headstone ordered. But I didn't get any of those marble vases. You know how bad they look — they've either got dead flowers in them or they're empty, and it looks like nobody cares. Speaking of, when are you going to put some flowers in the vases on Johnnie's grave?"

I was no longer listening. Instead, I had sat there, dumbfounded, picturing my destiny with Sam as my forever neighbor — telling me, for all eternity, that I was getting old or that I was doing something wrong. I knew the deceased didn't relocate all that often, but I began to entertain thoughts of digging Johnnie up that very afternoon and finding him — and us — a new home. Either that, or I would have myself cremated and leave instructions for someone to scatter my ashes far, far away — someplace where Sam could never find me.

Steeling my mind against thoughts of sprinkler systems, fences, and effervescent neighbors, I shook myself back into the present and drove home — only to face another onslaught of questions about my big lunch excursion. The girls jumped onto my bed and clamored for details. As much as I wanted to entertain them, I couldn't bring myself to relive the experience.

"I am not dating anymore," I said, sinking into the pile of pillows against my headboard. "I am going to start collecting cats."

"Oh, no, you're not!" Madison countered. "You've got to fix yourself up and get back out there. I mean — just look at yourself. No wonder you had such a bad date. Couldn't you wear something a little more … stylish? You look like a mother."

"I *am* a mother!" (Good Lord, was there no grace or mercy to be found?)

"Let her alone!" Jacquie hollered, fairly tackling Madison as she rummaged through my closet in search of something dateworthy. "She doesn't need to date anyway. She loved Dad, and she doesn't need to be with anyone else!"

Oh, boy. I could see where this one was headed. One vote for cat collecting; one vote for throwing myself at anything with an XY set of chromosomes. I needed a swing vote — and in it came, blue eyes shining and cheeks dimpling into a smile that lit up the room. "Hey, Aven," I said, scooting over to make room on the bed.

"What are we talking about?" our youngest wanted to know.

"Your sisters are discussing my social life," I said. "Or lack of one. What do you think I should do?"

"Well," Aven said, clearly pleased that her eleven-year-old opinion might matter, "I think you should do what you want. But we are not going to be here forever, so you might want to have someone to hang out with that you like besides a dog."

"Cats," I said. "Lonely old women have cats."

"Mom," Aven said with a smile, "you can do better than that. You are pretty. Don't listen to them — just try again."

And just like that, it was decided. I was headed back into the arena.

First, there was the guy who took me to the movies. I bought my own ticket. I told myself not to despair; perhaps Dutch treat had become the way of the world while I was off the market. But then I bought myself a large popcorn and a Coke — which he promptly devoured. I coined a term that night: "No repeater."

Then there was the guy who drank only water. No cocktails, no wine, no iced tea even. I went home that night and, per my mother's instructions, got out the whole bottle. Another no repeater.

Then came a string of men who mostly just wanted to have sex. On the first date. *For crying out loud*, I thought, *whatever happened to a kiss at the door?* Did none of these guys realize that I was old? Old people don't get into bed with just anyone. We might not have all our teeth, but we do have our standards.

No repeater, no repeater, no repeater.

(Ironically — and okay, somewhat pathetically — I found myself offended when the guys I'd nixed didn't call to ask me out again. I wasn't going to say yes, but I did think they might have at least called.)

Let's see. I went to dinner with a man who asked if I would sit in front of the TV at the bar so he could watch the game over my shoulder. I declined a date with a married man who offered to "help me out" in the intimacy department, if I just needed some action. And I suffered through an evening with a man who showed up wearing a fanny pack, told the chef not to serve him asparagus because it would make his pee smell, drank way too much, and wound up asking me — out of the blue, like "please pass the salt" — if men who'd had vasectomies could still get an erection, because he was thinking about having one. (*One of which?* I wondered. If I'd had a sharper knife, I might have offered to give him the former right there on the table.)

I began to grow wary of telephone calls, relying on caller ID to screen men whose names I didn't recognize. Even that plan, however, was not fail-safe. I saw an elderly gentleman's name, someone I recognized from the country club, and picked up the receiver. I'd seen the fellow at a memorial service the day before, and I was certain that, like others of his vintage, he was calling to ask me to prearrange his own funeral (a practice I highly recommend, by the way).

"Hi, Dee," he began. "It was good to see you yesterday."

"Thank you," I replied, happy to make small talk until he got around to the reason for his call. Nobody likes to talk about their own death; I wasn't going to push it.

"I thought maybe it would be nice if you and I went out for dinner."

Wow. I hadn't seen that one coming at all. Knocked off my game, I groped about for a ready excuse and, finding none, heard myself accepting his offer. The date was going fairly well — better, at least, than the fanny-pack man — until he asked me what I did for a living.

He had just seen me working a funeral; perhaps, given his age, he had Alzheimer's or some sort of dementia. "I work at H.D. Oliver," I reminded him. "Johnnie's business."

"You work at the funeral home?" He seemed stricken. "You don't get close to dead people — do you?"

"Well, that depends on what you mean by close." I laughed. "It's not like we have a *relationship*. I just send them off in the right direction."

My poor old date never recovered. I don't know whom he

thought he'd be dining with, but he definitely wanted no part of Morticia Addams. A no repeater.

It didn't take my friends long to realize I was never going to find a suitable bachelor on my own. Putting their heads together, they filled out a profile for me on one of those dating websites and launched me into the online world — one where everyone was attractive, personable, and unattached. (*If they're all that perfect*, I wondered, *why are they still single?*)

I woke up the next day and turned on the computer to find my list of potential soul mates. It was like Zappos, only better. I couldn't wait to get started.

The first guy to show up was so handsome that I had to pinch myself to be sure I wasn't dreaming. I wasn't. Not by a long shot. We'd barely said hello when he leaned into me and said, "I'm good-looking. You're good-looking. I would like to bed you down."

Excuse me?

Next up from the website was a man who must have been some sort of an anorexic. He didn't look skinny, but when the waitress came to take our orders and I asked for a salad, he said he'd share mine. Then I ordered some wine; he shared that too. We each got our own dinner (thankfully!), but when it came time for dessert, he informed the waitress that we were "full," but would she mind if he took the leftover bread home in a doggie bag? I said good night as soon as I could and headed over to my girlfriend's house, where a dinner party was in full swing. I pulled up a chair and tucked in.

Finally, though, my doctor arrived. All my life, since even before I'd met Johnnie, I had wanted to date a real doctor. They seemed so ... sexy. And responsible. And accomplished. I would, I was sure, feel very safe with a doctor at my arm.

We had a lovely evening — he even brought his own expensive bottle of wine to the restaurant, a move my mother would certainly have chalked up in the "plus" column — and then, just when I was beginning to think he might be my first "repeater," he leaned into my ear and whispered, "Do you want to play doctor?"

Had he really said that? Out loud?

I wasn't sure how to reply, so I just blurted out the first thing that came to my mind: "Um, no. Do you want to play funeral director?"

Later that night, as I lay alone in my bed, I found myself slipping into despair. I can spin a joke out of almost anything, and I certainly had plenty of comic fodder on the romance front. But honestly, I was getting weary of trying.

Even as I lay there, staring up at the ceiling, I sensed a comforting presence. I rolled over and grabbed my Bible off my nightstand — I'd taken to keeping it handy in the months since Johnnie'd been gone. I flipped it open to a random page, and my eye fell on Deuteronomy 33:12: *Let the beloved of the* LORD *rest secure in him, for he shields him all day long, and the one the* LORD *loves rests between his shoulders.*

I didn't remember ever seeing that verse before, but I felt like, somehow, God meant it just for me. He was letting me know I could rest, that he would be my shield. I didn't have to worry about dating or not dating; I was his beloved, and in that knowledge, I was secure.

I drifted off to sleep with a newfound peace. I wasn't sure if it would last forever, but it sure felt good that night.

And if things got really desperate, if ten more years went by without any solid prospects, at least I had a standing offer from Sam.

THE HOOD ORNAMENT
GETS A LICENSE

*T*here is only so much reality television a person can watch before real reality hits. Eventually, I knew, I was going to have to face the stack of papers that now covered the desk in Johnnie's once-tidy home office. Given the tardiness with which I paid the bills — with which I *found* the bills — it was a miracle that the girls and I still enjoyed modern conveniences like electricity and running water.

Fortifying myself with a bowl of Cheerios, I bellied up to the desk and began the sorting process. Cable, gas, power, Nordstrom, phone, newspaper, another Nordstrom (they are nothing if not patient), alarm company ... ugh. This could take a while. I realized I might need something a little stronger than Cheerios. Lucky Charms, maybe.

Suddenly, a couple of unusual papers caught my eye. Pulling them from the stack, I realized I was looking at a college application. My pulse quickened, and I had that strange feeling you get when you think you've had some sort of a premonition and now it's coming true.

Two years earlier, Johnnie had suggested I go back to school and get my mortuary degree so I could be licensed as a funeral director. That way, he said, I could serve as "backup." Like a cop, or something. "So what do you think?" he asked.

"I think," I said, "you're crazy. I am not going back to school."

"But, Dee," he said, pressing me. "Think about what a difference you could make. Right now, every time a family walks through our doors, you have to come find me or one of the other funeral directors. If you had your license, you could help them all by yourself."

"I don't mind working next to you, Johnnie," I countered. "I think we make a great team. And if I got a license, you'd probably have to pay me in something besides shoes.

"Besides," I continued, pulling out what I thought would be my trump card, "I don't have time to get another degree. We have three children, remember?"

"I know it would take time, but would you at least think about it? Not to be morbid, but at the rate we Olivers die off, it would be handy to have an extra Oliver on staff who was fully licensed."

Johnnie had a point. The Oliver men did not, as a rule, live all that long; his father had barely started collecting Social Security when he died, and one of his brothers had passed away in his forties. It was true that my having a license would help, and not just because we needed another funeral director on the roster. By state law, I couldn't make funeral arrangements for, or even be alone with, a grieving family, and sometimes (particularly when the bereaved were friends of ours) it could get a little bit awkward. I would want to comfort our friends or show support, but if I stopped by their home by myself — without Johnnie or one of the other directors — it could be considered a breach of professional standards. It was easy to understand why Johnnie had suggested I get my license.

Still, though, I really *hadn't* had time. And now it was too late. Johnnie had been right. Another Oliver was dead. Maybe they did need backup, but I wasn't about to step into the gap. Not with my world still reeling.

And so I had done the only thing I knew to do. Two weeks after we buried Johnnie, I went back to my old job at H.D. Oliver, standing beside the licensed professionals as they offered advice, dispensed tissues, and signed contracts. Through it all, my heart ached. Johnnie and I *had* been a good team; now, I felt like one half of a pair of bookends. I steeled myself to get through each new funeral. It felt so strange, watching another family's grief and thinking, "You don't know me, but I know. I know." I hurt for them, and I hurt for me. And all I could think was, *Please, God, don't let me start crying or totally fall apart and wind up toppling into the grave. People will think we charge extra for that.*

Eight months and stacks of unread newspapers later (now that Dear Abby is dead, I really only care about the obituaries), I unearthed the application. This time, it felt as though the pages were challenging me, daring me to complete the form. I remembered Johnnie telling me he had spoken to the head of the mortuary school to let him know I would be stopping by. Of course, I never had — there were dinners to cook, homework to supervise, online shopping to finish — and now I wondered if the fellow would even know who I was. Should I try it? Would I be embarrassed?

I had mixed emotions. On the one hand, I didn't know any other forty-fifty-somethings who had taken to wearing college T-shirts, and I wasn't sure I wanted to be the first. On the other hand, I knew there were a lot of people — many of them our dear friends — who had been counting on Johnnie to be there for them, and the fact that he was gone would not stop them from calling our home if and when they lost a loved one. I know I am no John Oliver, but maybe he had been right: Maybe if I had my license, I could be more than just a sympathetic ear; maybe I really could help.

Like most firms in the funeral business, H.D. Oliver employed very few women, but that didn't worry me. Johnnie had always made me feel welcome — even necessary. He knew that, license or not, a woman's presence during a time of grief or loss could make all the difference, and he jokingly referred to me as the "hood ornament." He was more than willing to be the car — to drive the whole operation — but as he saw it, if he had a wife who could dress things up and make the whole funeral planning process a little less intimidating or austere, then all the better.

I eyed the paperwork. I realized that, in going back to school, I would be stepping out of my comfort zone — and I wasn't sure how Johnnie's brother, Morty, would perceive the move. He had never invited me to work alongside him like Johnnie had; he had just sort of tolerated my presence, the way men do when their wives bring home a new lamp or a throw pillow they didn't know they needed (and that they are not entirely certain they like). Surely, though, Morty could use an extra pair of fully licensed hands — if, that is, I made it that far.

The application didn't look all that complicated.

I decided to go for it. If nothing else, I could take satisfaction in knowing I was doing something Johnnie had wanted me to do. And if everything went the way he had said it would, I could keep up the work we had done so well together, and in so doing, I would be able to honor his legacy.

First, though, I knew I'd have to pass organic chemistry. As if.

The whole endeavor seemed destined to fail. Hoping to avoid an embarrassing torrent of "I told you so's" if and when my academic career went south, I kept my enrollment plans to myself, telling only the girls, my father, and Sam. I left my Tory Burch satchel at home and borrowed a book bag from Madison, thinking it would help me blend in with the other coeds.

Right. I walked into class on Day One and realized, to my horror, that I was not only older than all of the students; I was older than the teacher. And not just by a birthday or two.

Tucking my chin so my hair hung down over my face, I slipped into the second row and sat down. I should have gotten some Botox. Heck, I should have dipped my entire body in the stuff. Better yet, I should have just gotten embalmed so nothing would jiggle or slip. I had never felt so out of place in my life.

The teacher began speaking. "I am Mrs. Whatever." I feel certain she said her name, but I couldn't hear it for all of the blood rushing through my ears, making the room sound like an oncoming freight train. To make matters worse, I realized I was sweating — and not just a little bit. Could I have hit meno-pause that quickly, without any warning?

Oblivious to my distress, Mrs. Whatever was still talking. "As you can see on the board behind me," she said, pointing to a series of letters and numbers, "I have a couple of simple problems to get us started today. Go ahead and get out a sheet of paper and work through them now."

Paper. Did I have any paper? I rooted around in the book bag. I had my calendar, with all of the information about my next garden club meeting and my upcoming hair color appointment and a starred reminder to call Aven's orthodon-tist (Shoot! That was yesterday!), but no actual paper.

"Excuse me," I whispered to the girl sitting next to me, "but do you have any extra paper?"

She looked at me like she'd seen the ghost of her grand-mother. If she was frightened by my wrinkles, I was equally taken aback by her tattoos. The girl was covered in ink. I don't mean just a butterfly or two; I mean covered like her pen had exploded up and down her arms, with what looked like drag-ons and flowers and mysterious signs whose origin and mean-ing I didn't want to begin to contemplate. It was all I could do not to blurt out the first thing that came to my mind: *Does your mother know you've done that?*

Instead, I flashed her what I hoped looked like a reassuring smile, and she handed me a piece of paper. White, pristine, unmarked paper.

Dee Oliver. There now. I had written my name. That wasn't so hard. I looked at the board and copied the problems, taking care not to juxtapose any numbers or omit any signs. All around me, students (I couldn't really think of them as my "peers") scribbled away, calculating and solving and generally making what looked like very good progress.

At the end of class, Mrs. Whatever collected our papers — mine with just my name and the unsolved equations — and gave us our assignments for the next class. I filed out with the crowd and went straight to my car. *Is it too late*, I wondered, *to ask for my money back?*

I sank down behind the wheel, and still in the parking lot, I picked up my cell phone and called my dad.

"I can't do this!" I said when I heard my father's voice, trying hard to be a big girl and not cry. "I had no idea what was going on in that class. I think it was chemistry, but it might have been Chinese. I quit!"

"Don't quit," he said soothingly. "I will help you. Bring your homework by the house, and we can look at it together."

I felt like a middle schooler, but I knew my father's offer was golden. A gifted mathematician with an engineering degree, he was as comfortable with science as I was at Saks. Cheered by the promise of his help, I resolved to go back.

I should have stopped my train of thought right there, but I couldn't help myself. I felt so alone. I wanted to talk to Johnnie, to tell him all about my first day. He would have loved the tattoo girl, as well as the African-American fellow who looked like a linebacker and told me I was too pretty to be in school. And the heavily pierced boys and the pregnant girls — when did organic chemistry start looking like a Lamaze class?

I stared out the windshield of my car. The girls were at school (as they should be, given the fact that, unlike their mother, they were all still young enough to be there). The only other person I could think to call was Sam.

"How the heck was it?" he hollered into the phone, seeing my name on his caller ID.

I couldn't answer for fear that my voice would break. I so wanted to be able to get my degree to make Johnnie happy, but I wasn't at all sure I could do it. In fact, I was pretty sure I couldn't.

"Hello?" Sam said again.

"Oh, Sam!" I wailed. "I can't do it! I am so stupid and old."

"You are not stupid," he said. "Old, yes. Stupid, no."

"Thanks." I sniffed.

"You are welcome." Through the phone, I could hear him grinning.

"Dee," he continued, "you can do this. It's just the first class. You are not a quitter. Remember — winners never quit, and quitters never win."

I let out some sort of sob, which I guess he took as an invitation to keep talking.

"Look," he said, "one of two things will happen: you are either going to pass this class or you are going to fail it. No one knows, and no one cares."

I preferred my father's brand of encouragement, but I couldn't deny Sam was right. Nobody even knew I was signed up for the class. And it's not like my seatmate would tattoo "I'm with Stupid" on her forearm. (Even if she'd wanted to, there wasn't any room left.)

So I stuck it out. And ten weeks and almost as many tutoring sessions with my father later, I walked out of organic chemistry with an A. My first phone call was to Sam.

"See?" he crowed. "I was right! You *aren't* stupid! But you are still old."

Heady with success, I ignored the barb and enrolled in a full slate of classes. By day, I worked at the funeral home and went to school; by night, I joined the girls at the kitchen table as we all pored over our textbooks and homework assignments. Home-cooked meals became a thing of the past, but nobody minded. The girls relished the fact that I was now worried about my own grades, and we all developed a taste for restaurant food. It was a long haul, but two years and a bunch of anatomy, accounting, religion, microbiology, pathology, and other – ology classes later, I had my degree.

Now all that stood between me and my license was three thousand hours of internship work. Forget that I had already accrued about three million hours of real work in the funeral business; in order for my license to be approved, I had to secure a bona fide internship. Some of my classmates headed to the city morgue to get their hours. Not wanting to appear soft or elitist (well, any more than I already did), I kept quiet about my plan to work at H.D. Oliver, surrounded by friends and the plush comfort afforded by John Bayne, the decorator Johnnie had kept on retainer in case of a pillow emergency or something.

I couldn't wait to share my good news with Morty, who had no idea I'd gone back to school, much less graduated. I took the girls with me to the funeral home, where Sam greeted us with a giant bear hug and a whisper of congratulations.

"Where's Morty?" I asked.

Sam tilted his head toward the garage. "In there."

The girls and I made our way back to the big room where they'd first learned to drink Coke and ride tricycles. To most people, it might have looked like a place to keep hearses; to them, it was a giant playroom filled with happy memories.

"Uncle Morty," I began, "the girls and I have something to tell you."

Madison couldn't wait. "Mom got her mortuary degree!" she announced, like we'd won the lottery.

"Is that true?" Morty said, turning to me.

"It is," I confirmed. "I still have to get my hours, and I am hoping I can do that here."

"You can't."

"What?" I wasn't sure I'd heard Morty right. Or maybe he hadn't heard me.

"I said," he repeated, through clenched teeth, "you can't. I didn't need my brother to help run this place, and I certainly don't need you."

My world started to spin. I wanted to press Morty for details. Had I done something to offend him? To make him angry? We had never been particularly close, but we'd had a decent professional relationship, and I thought he would have been happy to have another licensed funeral director — a family member — on board.

I was desperate for answers, but I didn't want to have what was shaping up to be an uncomfortable conversation in front of the girls. Morty could be a powder keg, but he was, after all, their uncle. Their father's brother. He looked at me through narrowed eyes, and I could feel the heat in my body starting to rise. Knowing that my temper was, if anything, more explosive than Morty's, I turned on my heel and ushered the girls out of the room. I couldn't get out of the garage fast enough.

Hurrying down the hall, we passed one of the offices, where I saw the intercom and realized that the boys had overheard the entire conversation. I couldn't read their faces; clearly, though, it was an awkward moment. I was stricken, but I wasn't about to let the girls see my pain. And even in the haze of my anger, I had enough sense to realize that even though I had inherited Johnnie's share of the business, Morty was the new CEO. The decision was his. We'd been dealt a blow, to be sure, but blows were nothing if not familiar, and I figured God would just have to find a way to prop us back up.

"It will be okay," I said, shepherding them toward the door. "And I have a great idea. Let's get some ice cream."

INTERMENT INTERN

I put on a good face for the girls, but inside I was reeling. How could Morty turn me away? And where was I supposed to do my internship if not at H.D. Oliver? The city morgue? No thank you. I'd seen enough *CSI* to know that wasn't for me.

I had felt so certain that God wanted me to go back to school. Had I heard him wrong? Were all those classes, all those homework hours, all that wondering about getting my own tattoo so I could fit in with the other college kids just going to come to nothing?

I don't know a whole lot of Bible verses by heart, but one that stuck with me in the early months of my widowhood was Jeremiah 29:11: " 'For I know the plans I have for you,' declares the LORD, 'plans to prosper you and not to harm you, plans to give you hope and a future.' " The idea that God had a plan, and that it was a plan I would probably like, was one of the main reasons I could get out of bed in the morning. (Truly. And here's a tip: I learned that, if I went to the trouble of making the bed right away, I would be less tempted to crawl back into it and hide from the world once I got the girls off to school.) Back then, I didn't have a clue what the future held, and I could hardly plan dinner, let alone the rest of my life. It was good to know God had me covered.

And I was pretty sure that part of his plan to prosper me and not to harm me was to send me to mortuary school. At least that's what it felt like when I found the application on Johnnie's desk, and then when I started getting A's in my classes. How was I supposed to carry on Johnnie's good work if I couldn't even get in the door? Could I have been mistaken about the whole "good plan" thing? Had I missed a memo? A Post-it note?

The funeral business is a fairly close-knit industry. *If I can't do my internship at H.D. Oliver*, I thought, *maybe one of our competitors will take me in*. After all, I had more than twenty years of experience. Surely someone in town could use an "interment intern" with my qualifications. Not only that, but I had an iPhone full of names and contact information for some of the oldest, most socially well-connected people in Tidewater. Some I knew from Johnnie's and my civic involvement, from places like garden club and the Rotary. Some I knew from church. Some were just friends we'd picked up along the way. All of them were going to die at some point. Almost all of them were apt to want a "nice" funeral, and virtually every one of them had families that would probably call me first — some even before they dialed their minister or 911.

I was confident that if Johnnie's brother didn't want my Rolodex, someone else would.

I was confident, but I was wrong. According to the grapevine, nobody wanted to take me in for fear of stepping on toes at H.D. Oliver. Whether that was true I don't know; it didn't really matter. What mattered was that I had nowhere else to turn, and I was beginning to lose hope. The words of Jeremiah 29:11, once such a comfort in my time of loss, now almost seemed to mock me. If this was God's plan to "prosper" me, I would hate to see what he had up his sleeve when the time came to knock me down a peg or two.

I began to explore other options. I thought about running for city council but decided to start smaller when someone asked if they could nominate me to be on the vestry at Galilee Church. I agreed to put my name on the ballot — and lost.

Next, I hosted one of those home-show jewelry parties, the kind where the sales consultant wants you to sign up for a glamorous career as a stylist. I wound up with about $1,000 in free costume jewelry — and no desire to see an earring ever again.

Finally, in an effort to feel like I was contributing to *something*, I agreed to speak to a women's Bible study. They wanted to hear my story — what it was like to have to call the rescue squad in the middle of the night, to lose my husband so suddenly, to find myself alone with three young daughters to raise, and to try to find God's faithfulness in the midst of it all. I worked on my talk for two weeks, and I had to admit it was pretty good. It was honest, vulnerable, and full of what I considered to be some very sound advice. At the end, though, when the time came for audience questions, only one woman — who looked to be at least seventy-five — raised her hand.

"Can you tell us a little more about the Botox?" she said. "I mean, like where exactly do you put it?"

Needless to say, my search for meaning in life — to feel like I had a purpose — was not bearing much fruit. I was wondering whether I should change my tack and pack up the girls for a weekend at the Ritz with some therapeutic shopping at the Tysons Corner mall when my phone rang. It was Andrew, an attorney I knew who knew Everybody who was Anybody (as well as pretty much everybody who wasn't).

"Are you still trying to get that mortuary internship?" he asked.

"I guess so," I said. "I mean, that's what I would *like* to do."

"Well, call my assistant," Andrew said. "She's going to set you up with Paul Riddick. He'll take you."

Andrew wasn't all that funny of a guy, but this had to be some sort of joke. I knew Paul Riddick. Not personally, that is, but by name. And reputation. Everybody did. He owned a funeral home that catered to the African-American community in Norfolk. But that's not why folks knew him; they knew him because he was always cropping up in the newspaper, making headlines in one colorful story or another. A Norfolk city councilman and the former president of the city's chapter of the NAACP, he was a power player on the Norfolk scene. He had strong opinions, and he wasn't afraid to share them. According to one account, Riddick had actually thrown a package of sliced ham at a deli-counter clerk — a move that, having had my own little episode with the engagement ring, kind of endeared him to me. There aren't many of us who will part with something valuable — be it our jewelry or our lunch — to ensure that other people are paying attention.

"Ah, Andrew," I began, "I'm not sure that's such a good idea."

"Of course it is. I know Paul. He's a good guy."

"I am sure he is," I agreed. "But be that as it may, I'm pretty sure he isn't going to want a white woman working for him."

"Oh, he'll take you," Andrew said, warming to his pitch as though he were closing one of his multimillion dollar deals. "We go back a long way. Just call him."

With little else on my plate (the jewelry consultant was still Facebooking me to see if I wanted to have Another Fun Party!!!), I agreed to make the call. To my surprise — shock, actually — Paul Riddick said he had heard good things about me, and I could start whenever I wanted.

Somewhat dazed, I thanked Mr. Riddick for the offer and hung up the phone. I wasn't at all sure I should take the job. I figured that, once word got out, people — my people — would talk. I didn't know whether I cared or not (I am not, normally, intimidated by gossip; I have a sign outside my back door that says, "People will stare. Make it worth their while."), but before I could even begin to process my thoughts, the tongue wagging began.

"Did I hear," asked a neighbor at a cocktail party two nights later, "that you might be taking a new job?"

Like all good grapevine material, the question was left

purposely vague, the questioner no doubt hoping to elicit additional information from my response. Not wanting to give the rumor mill any more fodder than it already had with the tantalizing image of a widowed white socialite working in an all-black funeral home in a most definitely all-black neighborhood, I just smiled and said, "I might have." (And then, with a combination of speed and grace that would have made my dear mother proud, I slipped out of the party.)

I needed advice. Johnnie would know what I should do. Not for the first time, I found myself wishing for a hotline to his cloud bank.

I wanted to take the job, but should I? Could I?

When it comes to dead bodies, people are funny. And it's not just color; religion and culture factor into the mix just as strongly. White, black, or blue; Catholic, Baptist, or Buddhist; it doesn't matter. You can work alongside one another, go to school together, and even sometimes intermarry without anyone batting an eye, but when the time comes to bid this life farewell, people stick to their own kind. The funeral business is, hands down, the most culturally segregated industry in America. Nobody takes offense; it just is what it is.

Reluctant as I was to bridge the cultural divide, I knew I didn't really have any choice. I needed to take the job (and secure my internship hours) or risk losing everything I had worked so hard to achieve. Even so, I found every reason to postpone my start date.

First, school was scheduled to start in a few weeks. Never mind that my girls were all teenagers (and one was already in college!); I felt they needed me at home. How would they get dressed in the morning without my help? (The same way they had for years, but I wasn't exactly thinking straight.)

And then came Halloween. Who starts a new job when there is candy to buy and neighborhood children to ply with sugar?

Next up was Thanksgiving. Choosing the right organic turkey would, I knew, take some time, as would preparing to run (or walk) in the mayor's annual Turkey Trot. I needed to be able to focus; starting a new job would just be a distraction.

The fact that one should not jump into a new venture during the Christmas season goes without saying. And, as if all that shopping, wrapping, and baking a birthday cake for Jesus were not enough for one unemployed woman to handle, consider this: It was *Debutante Season.*

Jacquie, my eldest, was making her debut. If you've never had to dress a deb for The Season, let me just say that, unless you are Kate Middleton's mother and you have a staff of couture experts on call, you do not want to be working in a funeral home. Or really, in any job. Although I am sure that plenty of working women have shepherded their daughters through two months of tea parties, brunches, and Cinderella-style balls without wrinkling their Vera Wangs. But those mothers are better women than me.

Finally, though, January morphed into February, and with the girls back in school and spring just a few weeks away, I ran out of excuses. It was time to go to work.

But ... at a black funeral home?

I realized I hadn't run any of this by my father, a man

who hailed from a far more segregated generation than mine. Surely he would put the kibosh on my plan. Sensing my escape route, I resolved to seek his counsel. I drove over to his house.

"Dad," I said, "I have an offer to do an internship at another funeral home."

"Yes?" he said, waiting for me to continue.

"It's at Mr. Riddick's firm, the one in town. Do you know who I am speaking about?"

(By "town," he knew I meant Norfolk. Anyone who'd lived in Virginia Beach as long as our family had lived there knew that, despite two generations of residential growth, sprawling strip malls, and commercial development at the Beach, Norfolk would always and forever be where we went when we went "to town.")

"I do know Mr. Riddick," my father said. "As a matter of fact, he is on the front page of the newspaper today. Something about owing money in back taxes, I believe."

"That's the one," I said.

"Mm-hmm."

I couldn't tell what my father meant by that, but I took a guess. "So you think I shouldn't go there, then? I guess I could call Morty one more time and see if he'll have me."

At that, my dad smiled. "No, don't call Morty. I think Riddick would be a great job for you."

"You do?"

"I do. And it sounds like Mr. Riddick could use another friend right about now. Take the job."

And so I did.

PART
THREE

*You Have
Overcome Too*

WOMAN IN BLACK

I pulled up to Riddick Funeral Service on a gray and rainy morning. I sat in the parking lot and took stock of myself: black SUV, black suit, black raincoat, black umbrella. How had my life become so colorless?

I love blue. It's probably one more result of assiduous fashion coaching from my mother, who told me to "always wear blue" since it made my blue eyes "bluer." And I did wear a lot of blue — back in the day. Back, that is, before I met Johnnie. Who knew a man could affect your palette so powerfully?

I'll never forget the first time we went car shopping together. The car was going to be mine, and I pictured myself tooling around in a little blue sports car, which would showcase my eyes to their best advantage. And if I got a convertible, my hair would look good too. I'd never had a new car; it would, I figured, be the perfect fashion accessory, opening up a whole new world of aesthetic possibilities, and I wanted to choose the style and color carefully.

When I shared my thoughts with Johnnie, he shook his head. "Not blue," he said. "Black. All cars are black. Jet black."

Jet black? That sounded like a mascara, not a car. "But it is going to be *my* car," I said. "Why does it have to be black?"

"We might need it in an emergency."

I was twenty-seven years old at the time, and I couldn't imagine an emergency that would necessitate having a black car on hand. But Johnnie wasn't finished. Not only did my car have to be black, but it had to be an SUV because, he explained, "You have to have four-wheel drive in case there is a snowstorm or a hurricane and the hearses can't get out. And the car has to be long enough to hold a cot or a casket."

So I got a big, black SUV. And in the ongoing effort to be prepared, I also learned to wear black: black dresses, black coats, and black shoes. (I was ready to draw the line, however, had Johnnie ever asked me to deck our girls out in little, black smocked dresses. Even Morticia Addams would have considered that a little creepy.)

Once I got used to my new "signature color," I realized it actually made life simpler. And even after Johnnie died and I no longer needed to be ready to fetch a casket in a blizzard, I still picked black when the car salesman showed me his inventory.

And so it was that I found myself in a black car with a black dress on when I pulled into Riddick. As if to complete the outfit, I also had a black cloud hanging over my head. I love my dad and I respect his opinion more than anyone's, but as I sat there in the parking lot, I couldn't shake the fear that I was making a big mistake. Why had I ever thought that taking this job would be a good idea?

I noticed a woman on the other side of the lot. She had unlocked the gates on the far side of the wrought-iron fence and was now making her way toward me. As I climbed out of my car, trying to look more confident than I felt, she gave me a critical eye.

"May I help you?" she asked.

"Thank you," I said. "I am here to see Mr. Paul Riddick. He is expecting me."

Again, the woman looked me over. I fought the urge to look down to see if maybe my coat was on inside out or if I'd accidentally worn one navy blue pump (not likely, but not unprecedented). Finally she turned on her heel and walked away.

I stood there in the misting rain, unsure whether or not I was to follow. Fortunately, I didn't have to wonder long. "Ya comin'?" she hollered, looking back over her shoulder.

"Right behind you!" I said, hustling to catch up before she reached the door.

Once inside the building, she asked my name.

"I am Dee Oliver," I said somewhat proudly, certain that (in the funeral world, at least) the name would enhance my standing.

The woman's gaze didn't flicker. Clearly, she had never heard of H.D. Oliver or any of his kin. I could have been Little Bo Peep for all she cared.

"Mr. Riddick isn't in right now," she said, "but his son P.J. is. I'll let him know you're here."

With that, she disappeared, leaving me to take in my surroundings. I was in some sort of reception room. There was a fireplace, and on the mantel I saw several framed documents. Stepping closer, I realized they were business licenses, and there — right alongside Mr. Riddick's license and those of some other funeral directors whose names I didn't recognize — was mine. *Deona Branch Oliver. Funeral Intern.* It looked official.

Soon the woman was back.

"P.J. is busy right now," she said. "Please wait."

Not having anything else to do, I took a seat. The woman sat down across from me. I wanted to say something, to show her my license, to establish some sort of credibility, but I felt like a captive beneath her stare. Never mind Little Bo Peep; I was starting to feel like a lost sheep.

Finally she spoke.

"Are you from the IRS?"

I wanted to laugh out loud. I guess what with all of my black clothing, I might as well have been. "No." I grinned.

"Are you a reporter?"

That made me smile even more. If only she knew what an atrocious speller I was, to say nothing of my grammar. "No, I am not a reporter," I answered.

"Well, what are you then?" Clearly, I didn't look bereaved, at least not the way most of Riddick's clients — whom I assumed were primarily African American — would have, had they come to make funeral arrangements.

"Well," I said, returning her gaze and broadening my smile, "I think I work here."

"What?" the woman exclaimed, shooting out of her chair. *"Hell to the no!"*

("Hell to the no," I would later learn, was one of Yvonne's — for that turned out to be her name — favorite expressions, used in place of everything from "Excuse me?" to "You don't say!")

"Well, yes I do," I said, pointing at my internship license.

"Well, dang," Yvonne said, collapsing back into her chair. "What do you know about that?"

And that, I realized, was my official welcome.

The lack of fanfare heralding my arrival should have established my place in the pecking order, but I wasn't savvy enough to realize I didn't know what I didn't know. Embarrassing as it is to admit it now, I saw myself not so much as an intern at Riddick as sort of a benefactor. With all my years of funeral experience, taken together with my newly minted mortuary science degree, I figured I could pitch in wherever help was needed, and maybe even teach the Riddick employees a thing or two. Choosing a casket? Let me show you the options. The right outfit for the deceased? Easy. Unsightly bulges or sagging breasts? I'd witnessed miracles done with duct tape that you wouldn't believe. I didn't even flinch at the embalming process; I'd seen it done so many times and to such excellent effect that I half wondered whether I should try it at some point instead of that pricey and all-too-temporary Botox.

I definitely knew a thing or two about staging a tasteful funeral, and I looked forward to sharing my vast wealth of knowledge with my new coworkers.

Right.

Not a week passed before my grandiose, egomaniacal plans came to a screeching halt. Riddick was prepping for a funeral, and the deceased — an elderly woman with a whole passel of grieving relatives — had already been embalmed and laid out in her casket. Dressed in her funeral finery, she was now resting peacefully in the Riddick chapel.

Somehow, amid their collective grief, the family had forgotten to bring the woman's wig when they brought her clothes. Unconcerned, they'd dropped it off at the office after she had been placed in her casket, certain that someone would make the necessary adjustments. That someone, as it turned out, was me.

"Go put this on the lady's head," I was told, as one of the Riddick employees handed off the wig en route to a more important task. I opened my mouth to protest — I had never once tried a wig on my own head, let alone someone else's (living or dead), and I wasn't sure where to begin — but before I could say anything, the wig bearer was gone. Holding the hairpiece as if it were some holy artifact, I made my way into the chapel.

"Hello," I said, looking down at the nearly bald woman. Could I really do this?

It didn't seem right to just shove the hair on her head. Doing so would seem disrespectful. Taking the time to be tender, however, would feel far too familiar; we were, after all, perfect strangers. I decided it would be best to start with some sort of introduction.

"Ah, hello," I said again. "We have never had the pleasure of meeting, but I am sure you were — are — a lovely woman."

She did seem lovely. She had probably raised a whole bunch of children and led a long and memorable life filled with family dinners and Sundays at church, and now she was stuck with me for a hairdresser. I sincerely hoped she was busy doing something — hanging out with the angels, maybe — so she didn't have to watch me fumble.

"I'm sorry," I said, half hoping she might crack open an eye and help me out. "I am not really sure ..." I let my voice drift off as I nestled the wig into place and stepped back to admire my handiwork.

It didn't look right. In fact, I was pretty sure I'd put the hair on backward.

I tried again. And then again. And then finally, as I worked one of the curls into place over her ear, I started to laugh. I couldn't help it. I was an utter failure, and yet, somehow, I knew that my new friend — hairdressers and their clients almost always form strong bonds quickly — was laughing too. And when all was said and done, she actually looked pretty darn good. Beautiful, in fact.

I, on the other hand, was a mess. I'd taken off my jacket on account of the humidity, and the armpits of my dress were marked with sweat rings. My giggles had given way to tears, and my mascara had run down my cheeks. And my hair, normally brushed to a glossy sheen, stuck out all over the place as though I had just finished a workout.

Which, in some ways, I had. (There's a reason behind the term "dead weight.")

I looked at the woman, whose name I had never learned, and my heart swelled with love. I could just picture her in heaven, calling out to all of her girlfriends: "Come over here and look at this pathetic white girl trying to put this wig on my head!" And all of her friends would be there, along with a host of angels, and they'd be falling down among the clouds, just laughing at me.

I had a lot to learn.

WHAT WE
GOT HERE

*L*ooking out the big glass doors, I could see the first wave of mourners arrive, the sunlight glinting off of the smartly polished rims on their Cadillacs and Escalades. Summer had come early, and it was almost as hot inside the funeral home as it was outside. I was glad I'd chosen a sleeveless dress. Standing tall in my new Kate Spade pumps, I imagined that Paul Riddick would approve. I looked like a classy funeral director: The black attire set a dignified tone, yet the cut of my dress — with a hemline that fell, tastefully I thought, just above the knee — hinted at a certain understated elegance and grace.

I wished I felt as confident as I looked. I figured I'd hosted well over a thousand funerals in my day — Protestant, Catholic, Jewish, and Greek Orthodox — but this was my first black one.

"Here. Take these." I looked up to see Mr. Riddick's son, Paul Jr. — P.J. for short — holding a stack of what I quickly gathered were fans, the kind that look sort of like paper plates attached to double-wide popsicle sticks. "Give these to people as they come in. It's hotter than a pup in heat out there today."

I looked down at my stash. The fans bore the photographic image of the Riddick men: Riddick himself in the center, flanked by P.J., Isaac (Paul Riddick's son from another marriage), and a grandson, a young man whose name I did not know. Their faces were an inscrutable mix of professional gravity and familial warmth, a look that managed to convey sympathy and concern in a way that clearly said, "Welcome." It was, I thought, a stroke of marketing genius.

And, I soon realized, the fans were not just for show. P.J. opened the doors to welcome the bereaved, and my heart sank. Broad-brimmed hats. Long, flowing dresses. With generously cut sleeves. It didn't matter that the thermometer was inching toward the 95-degree mark; suddenly, my "understated elegance" looked out of place, and I longed for a sweater, or even a bathrobe, to cover my naked, lily-white arms and legs.

The sanctuary filled, and P.J. motioned me toward a pew in the back of the church, where I found a seat between Lil Charles (the part-time limo driver who also went by the name "The Governor") and Mr. Washington, whose first name I had yet to hear and whose other job, when he wasn't driving hearses or directing traffic for a funeral, was at a mall, where I gathered he worked as some sort of security guard. Not having anything to read — the family had not, evidently, reckoned on the popularity of the deceased, and we'd run out of programs — I busied myself with studying the gathered.

The men looked like they'd just stepped off the pages of a

magazine. Sharp suits, spit-shined shoes, and dapper hats gave them a collective air of confidence, as though by sheer force of style they could keep death at bay. Not to be outdone, the women were adorned with white gloves, feathered hats, and all manner of beads and jewels. And the shoes! I had never seen so many pairs of stiletto heels outside of a Broadway musical. How did they walk in those things? Did they wear them to the cemetery? I wondered how Johnnie would have felt about that. A stickler for lawn maintenance, he might have preferred that the women wear flats to walk across his grassy plots. Then again, the aeration potential afforded by these spiky heels was mind-boggling.

"Heaven is a prepared place for prepared people."

The minister's words interrupted my people watching. The crowd listened appreciatively — there were lots of "Amen!'s" and "Yes, Lord!'s" — but I wondered how much longer he planned to speak. He'd been at it for over an hour, and he had yet to even mention the deceased. The Presbyterians would have been into the third verse of "Amazing Grace" by now; the Episcopalians would be circling the ham biscuits and moseying toward the bar at the postservice country club reception. I snuck a peek at my watch.

"You can't be living a life of promiscuity. You can't be messin' around. You might think you are steppin' out — but watch out! You never know when your next step is goin' to be your last step!"

The man had a point. But I hadn't planned on sitting for so long, and nature was calling. I'd already seen one man get up to answer his cell phone, and with all the hand waving and clapping that was going on, I didn't think anyone would notice if I slipped out for a minute.

"Excuse me," I whispered to Mr. Washington, who tilted his knees so I could get by.

So much for stealth. As I neared the aisle, at least a dozen heads turned to look in my direction. I locked eyes with one gentleman and then quickly averted my gaze. In that briefest moment, I'd read his unspoken question. It was without malice, but with undisguised curiosity: *What is a white woman doing here?*

Looking into the restroom mirror, I asked myself the same thing. What *was* I doing at Riddick? Surely, it was more than just a testament to God's sense of humor. *Oh, Lord*, I prayed with a sigh, *I'm sure you know what you're doing. I just wish you'd clue me in too.*

When I returned to my seat, the minister's voice had gone up a notch in volume.

"God gives us free will from the cradle to the grave," he said. *"And the choices that we make make a difference. The greatest choice we have to make is to follow Jesus. And time is running out."*

Time, I thought, was definitely running out — at least for this particular service. Clearly, though, nobody else was concerned. Several people had gotten to their feet, like they were at a rock concert. I found myself captivated.

"People put Jesus off until it's too late. The worst thing you can do is put off Jesus and struggle by yourself, becoming weak

and powerless against the devil. If you got Jesus, then you got the best. Doesn't everyone want the best? Can I get a witness?"

"Yes, Lord! Amen! Dear Jesus!" Arms in the air, the crowd fairly roared its approval.

I found myself wishing my daughters could see this. They served as acolytes at Galilee, and the closest they'd ever gotten to this level of spiritual fervor was the time one of their peers (they never did out him) stole the incense burner and the Sanctus bells and hid them in the church attic — a move that sent the vestry into a tizzy and resulted in a costly bill from the local locksmith.

The funny thing was, I agreed with everything the minister had said. Jesus really *was* the best. He had seen my family through some pretty tough times, and we'd come out okay. A little battered, maybe, but definitely okay.

"You need to accept Jesus." The minister continued on, his rich voice booming over the crowd. *"Don't think that havin' money or cars or a big name or even children — as big of blessins as they are — will save you. Just come on forward and tell Jesus that you want him to be your Lord and Savior. It's time to choose!"*

The churches of my upbringing — first Catholic and then Episcopalian — hadn't been all that big on audience participation, so I was startled when three or four people left their seats and made their way down the aisle. *Wow*, I marveled. *He actually got some.*

Clearly, though, the minister wasn't satisfied with this paltry harvest.

"I know there is someone else out there, and God is tuggin' at your heart. All you have to do is say yes. Just accept Jesus."

No one moved. The minister waited, and after a few more minutes it seemed to me that everyone there had either (1) accepted Jesus already or (2) was not planning to do so that day. I glanced again at my watch. An hour and forty-five.

When I looked up, I noticed a few heads swivel my way. And then a few more. Suddenly, it became strikingly obvious. They were waiting for *me*. They wanted me to go forward!

I fought the urge to stand up and explain myself, to let everyone know that I had, in fact, "accepted Jesus," and that if my salvation was the holdup, well, we could just wrap this funeral up right then and there and head on out to the cemetery. Lil Charles had told me about the "repass" that came after the service — a reception that included all manner of culinary delights and to which, as far as I knew, I was not invited — and I was pretty sure he wasn't the only one whose stomach was growling. Maybe I should just go forward as a courtesy, both to the zealous minister and to his hungry flock.

Instead, I lowered my eyes and folded my hands, trying to appear holy and prayerful, and as little like a target as possible. Finally, I guess, they all gave up on me, because moments later we were on our feet, making our way toward the exits. I stepped out into the parking lot, ready to help direct traffic. The women tottered unsteadily toward their cars. The lady nearest me reached her vehicle, sank down on the front seat, and put her hand to the floorboards. In a flash, the stilettos were gone, replaced by a pair of large, incredibly comfortable-looking, plush purple slippers. Scanning the lot, I saw that virtually all of the women's footwear had been similarly transformed. Brilliant. I resolved to steal the fashion trick at my first opportunity.

"Excuse me, ma'am?" The gentleman who had looked at me during the service appeared at my side.

"May I help you?" I inquired.

"Are you a reporter?"

Caught slightly off guard, I hesitated for the briefest second. "No, I'm — that is, I work here. Well, not *here*," I said, waving my hand to indicate the church. "I mean, I work for Mr. Riddick."

"Really?"

"Yes, sir."

"So," he said slowly, chewing this piece of news the way a child might process his first lima bean. He wasn't sure whether or not to accept it. "So what we got here is a white woman working in a black funeral home."

"Yes, sir. That's exactly what you got."

"Well, then," he concluded, "I guess you have overcome too." And with that, he tipped his hat to me and walked away.

Watching his back, I couldn't help but smile. *Yes, Lord*, I agreed, my smile breaking into a grin, *I guess I have.*

LOOK AT WHAT THE
WHITE WOMAN GONE
AND DONE NOW

*A*s the weeks passed, I began to grow more comfortable at Riddick. I didn't see Mr. Riddick much; he usually gave me my marching orders early in the morning and then directed his focus to other people and problems that required his attention. But he didn't need to be physically there to make his presence felt: A broad-shouldered man with a ready smile and a booming voice, Paul Riddick left his mark wherever he went. He knew more about Norfolk history than almost anyone I'd ever met, and as I watched him interact with the grieving families that found their way to his establishment, I soon grew to respect his wisdom and his warmth. Rarely had I known anyone so quick to extend a helping hand or so ready to offer strength and protection in the face of poverty or injustice. I found myself wanting to call the newspaper — the reporters who covered things like his IRS problems, his racially tinged language, and his ham-throwing antics. "You only have half of the story," I would say. "Come sit in my chair for a while; you'll see who Paul Riddick really is."

By "my chair," I meant the red velvet wing chair in the windowless room where I spent much of my time. They hadn't given me any sort of "official" place to work, so I'd ensconced myself in a room that, from what I could tell, served two main purposes. It was a viewing room where the bereaved could spend some private time sitting comfortably with the deceased (which accounted for the aforementioned chair and matching Victorian-era sofa), as well as a storage locker of sorts (a stack of metal folding chairs took up a good part of the room). I also had access to a reading lamp, a pile of brochures featuring photos of the Riddick men, and a Bible. All in all, it was not a bad place to hang out.

Yvonne, who had introduced herself as the housekeeper, was quickly becoming my best friend. She referred to the viewing room as my "office" and popped by whenever she had a free moment. A big-hearted woman who loved fishing, crabbing, and football (she had sweatshirts to honor both the Dallas Cowboys and the University of Virginia and wore them on alternate days), Yvonne had earned the nickname "Miss Utilities" from Mr. Riddick — and from what I could tell, it fit. In addition to cleaning the place, she knew how to repair whatever broke in the building, wash the funeral home's cars, and slap a coat of paint on pretty much anything that needed it.

Which is actually how we first got to be friends. I'd been

working at Riddick for about three months when I pulled up one day and saw Yvonne putting a fresh coat of paint on the black wrought-iron fence that borders the street side of the funeral home's property (the other three sides are marked by chain-link fencing). She had a cigarette in one hand and a paintbrush in the other, and her shirt was marked with perspiration. I checked the thermometer on my car. It was 98 degrees outside. I turned around and headed to the nearby Walmart to grab a Coke for her.

"Thanks," Yvonne said when I returned, reaching for the drink. "I gotta take a break anyway. I'm 'bout out of paint."

"I can go get some," I volunteered. The duties associated with my internship had been fairly loosely defined, and I was eager to be of service in any way I could.

"Okay," Yvonne agreed. "But I better ride with you so you don't get lost."

Tamping out her cigarette, Yvonne climbed up into my SUV. I was grateful for her company; I had no idea where the paint store was and didn't relish the idea of cruising up and down unfamiliar streets in a neighborhood where I was probably the only white person — the only white *woman* — within miles. I'd spent a lot of time in Norfolk, but Riddick's neighborhood, marked by fast-food restaurants, a dollar store, and a couple of gas stations that catered to the nearby interstate traffic, was uncharted territory for me.

We got back with the paint, and having nothing else to do in my windowless office, I grabbed a paintbrush and started working alongside Yvonne. I couldn't help but wish that Johnnie could see me; he would have been so impressed! I knew he would have hired a painting contractor to do the work. Heck, he probably would have called the decorator to be sure we'd chosen the right shade of black for the fence.

It was hot, and I'd never painted a fence before, but I quickly got the hang of it and was mentally congratulating myself on my smooth transition from princess to painter when I felt my foot hit something. I looked down and saw the full gallon of black paint, tipped over and spreading an inky thickness across the parking lot.

"Damn!" Yvonne said, sounding more amused than angry. "Look at what the white woman gone and done now!"

It was the first time anyone at Riddick had mentioned race, at least in front of me. I looked at the grin spreading across Yvonne's face and knew I'd found a soul mate.

"I'll go get some paint thinner," I said with a sigh. "And you don't need to come with me — I'll be all right."

We finished the fence. Inspired by our success, we tackled the bathrooms the next week. I didn't need Johnnie's decorator to tell me they could use more than a fresh coat of paint.

"Isn't there a dollar store across the street?" I asked.

"That's right." Yvonne nodded.

Within moments, the two of us — feeling like a reality TV version of Thelma and Louise — were roaming the aisles, looking for tasteful accents. We settled on some artificial flowers, and using my considerable garden club expertise, we quickly had two new arrangements for the lavatory sink areas.

Yvonne and I were on a roll.

"What?" Yvonne said, as we stepped back to admire our handiwork. "I can tell you're thinking something."

"I can't figure out what's going on with this floor," I said, eyeing the patchwork linoleum. "It's like whoever put it in used three different types of flooring."

"They probably did." Yvonne shrugged and lit a cigarette.

I raised an eyebrow. "I thought you said you had to quit smoking."

"I said the *doctor* said I had to quit. I didn't say *I* said I was gonna quit. I can't."

"Yvonne," I said, meeting her eyes, "I've only known you for a couple of months, but I can tell you that you're one of the strongest women I have ever met. And the hardest working. If anyone can kick the habit, you can.

"And trust me," I continued, "I know a thing or two about smoking. It's one of the things they teach you in Catholic school. You show up on the first day, and they give you a uniform and a starter pack of Marlboro Lights."

I stopped by Costco on the way home that night to buy Yvonne some nicotine gum and hard candy. And, thinking about the bathrooms we'd just painted, I called a friend who owns several hotels. "Can you help me find some inexpensive flooring?" I asked.

He could, and as it turned out, he also had several reams of carpet taking up storage space in one of his warehouses. Could I, he wondered, use any of that?

The carpeting at Riddick was threadbare in spots and coming apart at the seams. I seized the hotelier's offer and called Yvonne. Yes, she said, the fellows who worked at the funeral home could lay down any carpet I could find. They also knew how to replace ceiling tiles; did I have a way to get some of those? The ones at Riddick were broken and water damaged.

I had noticed the unsightly tiles, but had held my tongue, fearing that if I criticized them, I would look even snootier than I probably already did. Now, though, since Yvonne had broached the subject, I couldn't help but ask the question that had been tumbling around in my mind ever since I'd started working at Riddick.

"I can get some tiles," I said, "but answer me this. I know Paul Riddick is an important man — I mean, he's on the city council, right? And he was a bigwig in the NAACP, and he's gotten all these citizen awards, correct?"

"That's right," Yvonne said, proudly.

"Well, if he's such a big deal, why hasn't he replaced the carpet in his place?"

Yvonne's laughter burst through the telephone, making me hold my iPhone away from my ear. "Girl!" she said. "You think people care about *carpet*? People in this neighborhood, they know Mr. Riddick. They know he'd give them the shirt off his back — and he probably has, plenty of times. He'll do anything for anybody, and when he's done all his doin', there just ain't usually too much left over for stuff like carpet."

Thinking about what Paul Riddick had done for me — taking an unknown white woman under his wing and welcoming her into his family business — I realized that the holes in his carpet (along with the mismatched linoleum, the peeling paint, and everything else I'd seen as an eyesore) were not testaments to the man's stinginess; rather, they were markers of his generosity. Riddick, more than most, knew the value of money—and the importance of using it wisely.

Yvonne's voice interrupted my thoughts. "So … you can get the new tiles?"

"I can get the new tiles," I said. "In fact, nothing would make me happier."

Almost before I knew what was happening, the new décor had arrived, along with a small army of volunteers recruited by my friend Oz, the ruggedly handsome owner of a construction company who, I'd learned, could build or fix just about anything. Oz was one of the most generous people I'd ever met, and in less than half the time it would have taken Johnnie's decorator to stop by the funeral home with some swatches, the carpet went down, the ceiling went up, and we had a whole new look. *Extreme Makeover*, eat your heart out.

Yvonne and I hung photographs of the Riddick family in the living room area, over the fireplace mantel. They were, I thought, much more interesting than most of the pricey oil paintings that adorned the walls at H.D. Oliver. My favorite piece of Riddick "art" hung in one of the offices. It was the high school composite for Booker T. Washington, Class of 1956. Looking at the faces—not a white one among them—I couldn't help but wonder where these young men and women were now, nearly a half century after their graduation. So much had changed in the world.

And yet, in the funeral business, so much had stayed the same. Blacks and whites had kept their fences up, at least when it came to being buried. All too aware of the unspoken barrier our culture had hung between us, I was increasingly grateful for the way Paul Riddick, P.J., and Yvonne had welcomed me not just as a business associate but also as a friend.

Every time I turned around, it seemed, they were doing something to brighten my day. Yvonne made sure my car stayed spotless — I had never seen the rims look so good — and P.J. took care to show me the ins and outs of the building. Neither of them made any apologies for the neighborhood; rather, they simply stressed the importance of keeping the cars and the building locked.

Locking my car was one thing; locking up the funeral home was another. Riddick is a sprawling establishment; two different buildings (one with an attached garage for the limos and hearses), plus a parking lot, make up the complex. The first building houses Paul Sr.'s office, a business office, and the "selection room," where forward-thinking clients or their bereaved families can choose from among a wide variety of caskets, urns, and mock vaults. (A vault is the concrete box required by most cemeteries. It goes into the grave first, like a liner, in order to keep the ground level above the casket and protect it from dirt and moisture.) In addition to choosing a casket's exterior finish (metal or wood, in various grades and types), shoppers have a wide menu of interior fabric colors, embroidery choices (e.g., flowers, praying hands, an American flag), and other specialty options, ranging from secret drawers for mementos, to places to insert military insignias, to personalization possibilities like a family photo collage or a collegiate logo so you can display your school spirit for all eternity.

The other main building at Riddick is home to Paul Jr.'s office, the viewing and family visitation rooms (including the one in which I'd taken up residence and had grandiose plans to redecorate), the embalming room, and the chapel. Before Paul Riddick appropriated this second structure for his business, it had served as an area nightclub, which explained the smoky bronze-colored glass entrance hall that stretched the length of the building. The whole enterprise functioned a little bit like a rabbits' warren, with plenty of entry and exit points, but it worked. And it wasn't long before I knew my way around.

One day, during a particularly slow week, we got a "house call." I knew what that meant: someone had passed away at home, and they'd asked Mr. Riddick to send one of the funeral directors to collect the body. In this particular case, the family wanted to come to the office later that afternoon to meet with Mr. Riddick and make service arrangements.

As the day wore on, with nothing much happening, Mr. Riddick called over to my building to let me know it would be all right for me to go home, that he would wait for the family. Paul Jr. was out running errands, so the locking up fell to me.

I first secured P.J.'s office and the embalming rooms, using a key that was kept in a secret spot. Next, I darted across the parking lot to my car to stash my purse and other items while I went in search of the keys to the exterior nightclub doors.

I made sure to lock my car, and then I hurried back across the lot and slipped into the garage, grabbed the keys from Mr. Riddick's office, went back out the garage, crossed the lot again, locked up the nightclub, and then reversed the whole process, returning the keys and taking care to lock the garage door behind me. The whole operation took less than ten minutes, but I was out of breath from all of my dashing about.

Relieved to be heading home, I put my car in gear. Suddenly, out of the corner of my eye, I noticed a strange car in the parking lot, just outside the former nightclub entrance. Where had that come from? It didn't belong to P.J., and Yvonne had already left for the day. I looked back at the building. With the smoky glass, I couldn't see a thing. Was it possible that someone had entered the premises while I had been doing my wind sprints?

I didn't think so, but I had to be sure. Mr. Riddick's car was on the far side of the lot, and I knew, because I had just seen him when I dropped off his keys, he was in his office. Should I go and get him?

No. I was a big girl. I could handle this. I put my car in park and left it running (without locking it, which I knew would have given P.J. a fit) while I walked cautiously toward the entrance. Had I detected movement behind the murky glass?

Now I was at the door. I leaned into the glass, cupping my hands around my eyes to cut the glare — and jumped! There, mere inches away, were four bewildered clients, their eyes wide and their hands pressed against the glass. "We are locked in," they cried. "Let us out!"

Oh. My. Gosh. I had locked these people in the funeral home — in the embalming side. And I had no way to let them out. They were trapped!

"Hold on!" I yelled. "Don't go anywhere." (As if they could.)

Ignoring my car (which was still unlocked and, thanks to Yvonne, very clean and therefore very inviting-looking for any passing thieves), I ran around to the funeral home's front entrance, knowing no one was going to hear me if I stopped to bang on the garage doors. I rang the doorbell and began pounding on the woodwork.

As I raised my arm to pound again, the door suddenly swung open, and there stood Paul Riddick — all 6 feet, 225 pounds of him.

"Mrs. Oliver!" he boomed, giving me his standard enthusiastic greeting and deftly sidestepping my fist, even as his eyes scanned the street for any sign of trouble. "I thought you had left."

"I did," I said. "At least, I started to. But then — may I just have your keys, please?"

"My keys?"

"Yes. You know that family you've been waiting on? Well, I believe I have just locked them inside the other building."

Mr. Riddick reached into his pocket and handed me his keys, and then, rabbit-like, I dashed around to the other entrance and fumbled with the lock.

"I am so, so sorry," I said as my captives hustled out of the building.

"I have worked in the funeral business for more than twenty years," I blathered. "I have locked up plenty of deceased people but never anyone who was alive. And never a whole family."

If they answered me, I don't remember what they said. All I could think about was getting them safely delivered to Mr. Riddick's office and then getting out of there.

Driving home, the absurdity of it all hit me. Why did I bother watching television? My life, giant mess that it was, was so much more entertaining.

The next day when I arrived at work, Mr. Riddick had a gift waiting in my office. There, right next to the Bible, was my very own set of keys.

THE HORRIBLE MAN
HOMILY

*T*he weeks passed quickly at Riddick, and almost before I knew it, I had accumulated more than half of the three thousand hours I needed to log to complete my internship. I began mentally willing the days to drag on, as I wasn't ready to say good-bye to my red velvet chair or the friends I'd made.

Yvonne had been nicotine-free for eight months. I lost count of how many times my phone had rung — usually on weekends or at night when I was curled up against the down pillows on my bed — and her name would pop up on caller ID.

"I think I need a cigarette," Yvonne would say.

"Hell to the no you don't!" I would counter, tweaking her favorite expression as I eyed the clock on my bedside table and tried not to yawn. "You've come this far. Don't go back now. Have a Jolly Rancher."

I was so proud of her. Her wheezing had stopped, and she said the doctor had even noticed an improvement in her vascular problems, whatever those were. Yvonne's beloved Wahoos were still losing up the road in Charlottesville, but she had gained enough yardage in her own life to claim a personal victory. I never wanted to leave that woman.

Fortunately, I still had several months to go. And we had a big funeral on the docket, which always made my job even more interesting. I'd grown accustomed to the stares of our African-American clients (and yes, I'd begun to think of them as "our" clients) when they saw my white face sitting with the Riddick men in the chapel or directing traffic after a service — a skill I had perfected under Johnnie's expert tutelage. Funeral traffic was, I realized, no respecter of persons, regardless of race or socioeconomic status. Cars were cars, drivers were drivers, and all of them needed someone to tell them where to go. Sometimes the sight of me standing in the middle of the road in my black dress and matching pumps led to some rubbernecking, but Mr. Riddick didn't care, and neither did I. We got the job done.

At H.D. Oliver, I had known, by relationship or reputation, at least two-thirds of our clients. Garden clubbers, Bible study devotees, country club tennis champions, local politicians, bankers — they all died, eventually. And in most cases, I could have told you whether those who eulogized them were padding the accounts a little (a common practice), a lot (less common, but not unheard-of), or to the point where friends and family members might wonder if they were, in fact, in the right place.

Not so at Riddick. Here I knew no one. As such, every funeral represented the opportunity to hear new stories, to connect with the bereaved, to get to know the deceased, even if in an abbreviated context.

This new funeral was no exception; I'd never heard of the man. Apparently, though, everyone else had. We'd barely gotten settled into our seats before the minister — a man who'd flown in from California for the occasion — began recounting Frank's attributes.

Frank was, it seemed, quite a drinker. And he was more than a little bit fond of women — "runnin' around with them all the time" was how the minister put it, I think. "And," he went on, shaking his head in what I took to be resignation, "Frank was not a good daddy to his kids."

I couldn't believe it. This sort of stuff was undoubtedly true of some of the folks who'd passed away in my part of town, but you would almost never have heard it openly discussed (unless you count comments like, "He always was a bit of a free spirit, bless his heart."). And I am positive you would never, ever have heard such an unvarnished assessment at a funeral — bless-his-heart or not.

I found myself riveted.

The minister had tacked. No longer was he talking about Frank; now his focus was on a "bunch of black guys hangin'" out on the street corner." Had I missed something? Did everyone know who these "black guys" were — or how they figured into Frank's story?

"The last shall be first, and the first shall be last."

That one I had heard before. I knew it was from the Bible — don't ask me where — and I clung to the verse like a lifeline, waiting to hear how the minister was going to bring this rambling litany to some sort of closure.

"Well, these guys were standin' there on the corner, waitin' for the boss man to come by and offer them a day of work. Some guys, they got there early. They got a set wage for the day."

This sounded familiar. I racked my brain for the context; was it a Bible reference too? I was pretty sure I'd never read about a bunch of black guys on the street corner, but I hadn't always paid the closest attention, so maybe it was in there somewhere.

"Later on," the minister continued, "a guy shows up and the boss man offers him the same wage for the day. And then even later, in the afternoon, a couple more guys start hangin' out on the corner. The boss comes by and picks them up, sayin' he will pay them too — the exact same wage."

By now, I wasn't the only one paying attention. Every eye in the room was fixed on the pulpit.

"And then" (and I had to give it to the minister; he knew he had us in the palm of his hand), "Old Charlie shows up, late in the day, sayin' he need some work. The boss man picks him up too, because there is still work to be done at the construction site. There are only a couple of hours left in the day, but sure enough, Charlie gets paid the same wage."

The story was definitely ringing a bell. But still, it made me a little uncomfortable. I mean, why would Old Charlie get the same pay that the hardworking guys who showed up first thing got? It didn't really seem fair somehow.

Suddenly the minister interrupted my train of thought. It was as if he had read my mind. "Now, don't be getting into

Old Charlie's business," he said. "Don't be all worked up about that. You need to mind your own business, and let God worry about everyone else.

"You all can't be standin' in line," he continued, "peepin' out and lookin' at the guy in the front with the big ol' flat-screen TV or the shiny chrome rims on his Cadillac — just 'cuz you ain't got 'em on your car. You gotta be happy with what God's given you."

I wanted some time to process what I was hearing. I wasn't jealous of anybody's rims, but I felt like there was an important message in there somewhere. But the minister wasn't about to slow down; he was on a roll. And suddenly we were back to Frank:

"You can't be all bent outta shape here at ol' Frank, just 'cuz he was the last in gettin' right with the Lord. We all know he been drinkin' and chasin' women and never bein' much of a daddy to his kids. And he never did pay God any mind."

Ouch. This eulogy was definitely not like anything I'd ever heard before — at H.D. Oliver or Riddick or anyplace. Maybe in California, or wherever this guy had been trained, they placed a premium on honesty.

"And I know what you all are out there thinkin'. You're thinkin', *Well, I have been goin' to church and doin' what's good and it just ain't right for Frank to get the same reward I am gonna get when he showed up late.*"

I hadn't considered it in those terms, exactly, but I had to admit that the man was making sense. And, inexplicably, I found myself rooting for Frank. Clearly, he hadn't been a model citizen. Call me a champion of the underdog, or maybe it was just that I saw parts of myself in Frank, but I couldn't help but hope that he would somehow turn the tables on us all.

"But let me tell you somethin'." Here the minister leaned forward over the pulpit and lowered his voice, almost like he was daring anyone to voice a protest. "Frank accepted Jesus at the end. And that's Jesus' business, not yours."

With that, the eulogy ended.

I looked around. Everyone, it seemed, had been cowed into submission. Frank might have been a scoundrel in life, but he'd gotten an eleventh-hour ticket to heaven, and that was that. The last shall be first.

Later that night, I replayed the message over in my mind. I wasn't all that surprised by Frank's bad behavior; I'd known plenty of boozing philanderers in my day, many a lot worse than him. And really, I wasn't all that surprised by Frank's eternal fate. It matched everything I knew about grace.

What tripped me up — in a good way, I guess — was the realization that, at the end of the day, I wasn't much different. Snapping at my kids, lusting after *The Bachelor*, thinking mean thoughts about the neighbor's dog — I needed God's mercy every bit as much as Frank had.

I leaned back against my pillows and stared at the ceiling. I wasn't sure the whole "he was a horrible man" homily would go over too well in the Galilee pulpit, but from a purely evangelistic standpoint, it definitely had merit. Man's sin, God's grace.

Who could ask for anything more?

THE PROPHET
IN RED STILETTOS

*L*ooking back on the trepidation with which I had accepted the internship at Riddick, it was hard to remember what I had been so anxious about. Sure, working in a black funeral home was different, but as with any new adventure, it soon grew familiar. The garden clubbers had quit inquiring about my "new position," and life had settled into a fairly predictable routine. I woke up at 5:00 a.m. to spend some time with God and have a few quiet moments; then I got the girls up and fed and out the door to school; then I hopped in the car and went to Riddick, hoping to get a workout in either before or after work.

After so many months on the job, I'd been to all sorts of funerals, met any number of families, and learned the names of a good many clergy members. One day, though, the door opened and in walked a woman I'd never seen before. In fact, I couldn't remember ever seeing anyone quite like her.

She was a large-framed woman, and very tall, even if you

deducted four inches for the stiletto heels she was wearing. Red ones. Her hair was ironed flat and hung down around her shoulders, skimming the collar of her multihued dress. In her hands she carried a Bible and what I assumed were her clergy robes, although I wouldn't have sworn to it since my attention was much more focused on her fingernails, which were longer than any I'd ever seen and painted a deep, dark red — the perfect complement to her shoes.

"Do you work here?" she inquired, looking me over.

"Yes," I replied.

"Really?"

I wasn't surprised by her skepticism. Everyone who came through our doors had the same question. And they got the same answer: "Yes, I really do work here."

Satisfied, my visitor introduced herself. "I am the pastor. And I am a prophet. I hear from God."

I wasn't sure how to answer that, so I just smiled and waited for her to continue.

"Today is my wedding anniversary," she said.

"That's nice," I said. "Congratulations."

"Thank you. I would rather be spending the day with my husband — I had already arranged to take the day off — but then Cynthia's husband passed, and I felt it was my duty to come in and conduct the service."

"Well," I said, trying to be helpful, "I am sure the family will be very grateful. And when the service is over, you can go out and spend the rest of this beautiful day with your husband."

"Mm-hmmm," the pastor-prophet said, looking at me as though something had just occurred to her.

I waited a beat, but when nothing else seemed to be forthcoming, I pointed toward the ladies' room. "You can change in there," I said.

She emerged in full regalia, looking even more imposing than she had before.

"May I pray for you?" she asked.

I was surprised, but never being one to turn down a free prayer, I snuck a quick peek at my watch. I'd been to enough of the services at Riddick to know that these things could sometimes take a while.

"Well, yes," I said. "We have a couple of minutes."

The woman took my hands in hers, and I bowed my head. When she didn't say anything, I looked up, wanting to be sure I hadn't done something wrong. She was staring at me. "You know I am a prophet?"

For what felt like the umpteenth time since she'd walked through the door, I didn't have a ready answer. The only prophets I'd ever heard of were the ones in the Bible, and I generally pictured them as old white men with long beards. To say that she shattered my stereotype would have been putting it mildly.

"You mentioned that," I said.

With that, she started to pray, gripping my hands tightly in hers. I bowed my head again but opened one eye to peek. The fingernails seemed to be sprouting everywhere.

"You know," she said (and I wasn't sure if she was talking to me or to God), "the Bible says you reap what you sow."

I felt a shiver run up my spine. Just that morning — a matter of hours ago — I had said those very same words to Aven as we talked at breakfast about how she should behave at school and in her friendships. I'd given her a mini sermon on the benefits of sowing seeds of things like love and kindness and told her I tried to live my life that way. "It all comes back to you," I had said, "even when you are old, like me."

The prophet was still speaking, her words now definitely directed at me. "You have been sowing well," she said, "and you will see the goodness of what you have sown. You will reap it in your children, your work, your home, and in your old age."

I was floored. It was as if this giant red-heeled woman had been sitting at our breakfast table!

I looked up. Again the prophet was watching me. "Are you married?" she asked.

"No. I was, but my husband died a couple of years ago. His name was John Oliver."

"John Oliver?" the woman said. "Like from the big funeral home downtown?"

"The one and the same."

"Well, Mrs. John Oliver, you are going to get married again." She said it as plainly as if she'd said it would rain tomorrow, and then she looked away, and I realized she was praying again. Or maybe it was prophesying; I didn't know. I was way out of my league. My minister didn't do this sort of thing — at least not that I knew of.

"The Lord has a husband for you. But you don't need to go looking for him; he will find you."

The woman continued to pray, even when the phone rang, but I didn't hear much of what she said. I was focused on one word: *husband.* Did God really have someone for me? And was it true that I wouldn't have to troll the Internet to find him? A million questions ran through my mind, but for once I kept my mouth shut.

Finally, the prophet finished. "I am going to give you a Bible verse," she said. "I want you to pray it every day."

"Okay," I said with a nod.

"Joshua 1:8 – 9. 'Keep this Book of the Law always on your lips; meditate on it day and night, so that you may be careful to do everything written in it. Then you will be prosperous and successful.' "

I thought that sounded awesome, and I was just about to thank her, but she wasn't finished.

" 'Have I not commanded you? Be strong and courageous. Do not be afraid; do not be discouraged, for the LORD your God will be with you wherever you go.' "

I squeezed the woman's hands, too moved to speak. This sort of thing was probably an everyday deal for her, but I had never heard God's Word spoken that way — so personally and so directly. And with so much conviction.

"Thank you," I finally said, as the woman got up. The funeral was just about to begin, and she made her way toward the chapel.

I knew I would be needed in a minute, but I didn't want to break the spell just yet. I wanted to savor her words — God's words — and tuck them away in my heart. Of all the blessings

I'd been given during my time at Riddick, this one was, hands down, the best.

God, the One who held my future in his hands, had promised to be with me. And as if that weren't exciting enough, he might even bring a man along for the ride!

PART
FOUR

Can I Give You Some Advice?

THE BEST
LOVE LETTER EVER

*I*t's been more than a year since I finished my internship and stopped working at Riddick. I've stayed in touch with P.J. and Yvonne (who is still, I am happy to report, nicotine-free), and I still go back there sometimes. Mr. Riddick donated the red velvet furniture to an old lady who evidently needed it more than he did, but whenever I wanted a quiet place to study (I had to pass the state boards to get my funeral director's license, once the internship had been completed), he always found a spot for me to work.

If there's one thing I learned from my time at Riddick, it's that we're all basically the same. White or black, we're all going to end up in the same place (well, one of two places), but most of us don't like to think about death. And even fewer of us take the time to plan for it.

Which is kind of funny when you consider the odds of it happening.

By contrast, think about how much time we take planning

for other stuff. We talk to people, check out things on Google, and weigh our options on everything from the type of wedding cake we want to which career looks most promising. We analyze our health benefits, test-drive cars, and peek in the crawl spaces of our houses. When children come along, we buy books about what to name them, how to toilet train them, and what we should do when they announce that they don't need us anymore and they're leaving home to follow a rock-'n'-roll band. And don't get me started on pets! I spent more time researching what type of *dog* to get Johnnie for Christmas than I ever spent thinking about his casket — despite walking past it almost every single day (it was the one he would never let us sell, since it had a ding in the mahogany paneling).

Death is, perhaps, the only certainty in life that still manages to catch us off guard. And while browsing a headstone catalog (yes, they really have such a thing) over a glass of wine might not sound like a recipe for the perfect date night, taking time to address the small things (Does your wife know what all the keys on your key ring are for? Does your husband know how to make a pot of coffee, or even where you keep the filters?) and even the not-so-small things can make a big difference in how you will cope, should you one day find yourself in my shoes — dressed in black and sitting in the front pew, wondering how your life could have changed so fast.

Losing someone you love is never easy — and the advice I have to offer won't make it so — but my hope is that, by sharing my experiences (the things Johnnie and I did right, the things we did wrong, and the things we just plain forgot to address), I can help prepare and equip you for the journey.

And if you don't want to take advice from a television addict (and particularly one who has watched more than one season of *Who's Your Baby's Daddy?*), I understand. But don't be too quick to dismiss the benefits of tuning in to some of those late-night movies. You never know when you are going to pick up a valuable tip or discover some strategy that has real-life implications.

For instance, somewhere in the deep recesses of my brain there is an image of an envelope that was featured in one show or another. On the outside, written in large, black letters, was a message as ominous as it was intriguing: ONLY TO BE OPENED UPON MY DEATH.

I can't remember the details — maybe the letter contained the confession of a sordid love affair or an illegitimate child or the answer to an unsolved embezzlement scam or even a murder. What I do remember is that seeing the letter sparked an idea — and it's one I wish Johnnie and I had pursued.

Write your spouse a letter that is only to be opened upon your death. Ask him (or her) to write one too. Don't talk about secret affairs, stolen money, the whereabouts of a missing body (please!), or life's regrets. That sort of stuff, tossed out posthumously, can only cause confusion, heartache, or worse. Instead, devote your ink to the kind of information that no surviving spouse should ever be without.

Here's what I think Johnnie would have written to me, had we actually had the foresight to implement this plan:

My Dearest, Delightful, Darling Dee,

You have been the most important person in my life. You are the most beautiful, gracious, intelligent, fabulous woman I have ever met. Being with you made my life worth living —

Just kidding! Here's what he really might have written:

Hey, Dee,

Here is a list of the things you have nagged me about every single day. I didn't have time to mess with any of it, so I made one of the funeral directors at work do it for me. Hope this is everything. I love you.

Johnnie

And then, enclosed in the envelope, I would find:

- a list of the banks we do business with, along with account numbers and any necessary passwords

- information about any safety deposit boxes (along with where to find the key!)

- information about stocks, bonds, or other investments, as well as contact numbers for any brokers or fund managers

- the location of important documents, such as military discharge papers, birth certificates, marriage/divorce certificates, Social Security cards, passports, car titles, insurance policies, the deed to our home, tax returns, business agreements, and so on

- information about any business or real estate concerns about which I might not be aware

- instructions and information about how to access Social Security benefits

- the location of our wills (and please — if you don't have one, STOP READING NOW AND CALL A LAWYER. I'm no estate expert, but I do know that if you die without a will, the taxes, court costs, and other fees can siphon off as much as 70 percent of your assets! I tend to be a "silver lining" kind of gal, but there's not really a way to put a happy face on that)

- the names and phone numbers of our lawyer, accountant, life insurance company and agent, as well as contact information for other insurance policies

- passwords for any important websites

- the name and number of the funeral home we planned to use (Johnnie was nothing if not thorough, and he would probably have written "H.D. Oliver" in big, bold letters, lest a total stranger discover the letter before I did and ship him off to one of our competitors), along with the details of any prepaid arrangements we may have made and information about cemetery plots and the title deeds for those

- the location of his obituary (and while most people don't think to prewrite theirs, most surviving spouses or children wish they had!), along with instructions for submitting it to the newspaper

- any favorite Scripture passages or hymns he wanted to have included in his funeral service (as it was, I had to guess at some of this stuff — I sure hope he liked my choices)

- the name of the church or charity where he wanted memorial donations to be sent

And then, because Johnnie was an organized man, he would also have included a list of names and numbers for people I should notify about his death, particularly out-of-town friends and relatives. He might have even been savvy enough to add the names and numbers of our plumber, car mechanic, cell phone service provider, doctors, dentists, yard guys, babysitters, and the vet (although he would probably figure I had those last two on speed dial).

Does all of this sound like a lot? It is. But as with any of history's greatest love letters, it really is the thought — and in this case, the careful thought — that counts. Back when Elizabeth Barrett Browning penned her now-famous "How Do I Love Thee?" sonnet, she might not have numbered the location of her safety deposit box among the ways she counted, but when you get to the end of her poem, it seems clear she had a strong finish in mind. Envisioning a time when she and her beloved Robert would be separated, she vowed, "I shall but love thee better after death."

How many modern wives can say that?

Or, for that matter, how many husbands?

I sat with a man just the other day as he grieved the sudden death of his wife. And, given that she was the one who knew where everything was — from their wills to their address book — he found himself at a double loss. Moving forward without your life partner is hard enough; trying to do it when you don't have access to any information can feel practically impossible.

Write your spouse a letter. Seal it in an envelope. And then tape it to the back of your closet door — out of sight, but easy to access. (Oh, and tell a trusted friend what you've done, just in case you and your spouse go to the Great Beyond the way my friend's parents want to — en route home from a fabulous vacation in Bermuda, together when they are about 102 years old.)

Some secrets are better off taken to the grave. The name of your lawyer is not one of them. Tell your spouse. In the end, it really is just another way to say, "I love you."

WILLS, OBITS,
AND OTHER
ACCOMPLISHMENTS

*Y*ou might think that, having stood eyeball-to-eyeball with Death for more than twenty years, Johnnie and I would have dotted our i's, crossed our t's, and gotten ourselves more or less ready to follow Lord Tennyson across the bar. If you thought that, you would flatter me.

And you would be wrong.

Johnnie and I were no better than the vast majority of hale and hearty Americans who, statistically, spend forty or fifty years accumulating wealth — and *less than two hours* figuring out how it will ultimately be distributed. My own estate-planning expertise pretty much begins and ends with what I've picked up from Perry Mason and Judge Judy, but I do know this: If you care about what happens to your money when you die, you'll want to make a will. And to make a will, you'll want to hire an attorney. Don't just pick the first name that pops up on Google; get some recommendations from your friends and business associates. You'll want to find someone you and your spouse both feel comfortable with; after all, one of you will likely be holding his (or her) hand, at least metaphorically, at some point down the road.

After finding Johnnie's way-too-old will after he died — and realizing that mine was equally deficient — I had mine updated. I imagine there are very few, if any, people who actually like to spend time and money making a will, but it's kind of like getting a colonoscopy, I guess: You may dread it, but when it's over, you feel really good, knowing "that's done" and you don't have to think about it again for a while. And I love knowing that, should the time suddenly come for me to follow Johnnie, I will still be barking orders to my girls from beyond the grave. They'll know just what to do with the house, our bank accounts, and the portrait of my mother that hangs, seen by almost no one, in the formal silence of our living room.

And, to quote Forrest Gump, "That's all I have to say about that."

Obituaries, on the other hand, are fodder for a whole new conversation. There's an old joke in the funeral business where a guy opens the paper and says he knows it is going to be a good day when he reads the obituaries — and discovers his name isn't listed.

Actually, that's not much of joke. But then, neither is writing an obituary. For most people, it's an exercise fraught with pressure and uncertainty. It is the thing that everyone will read, and in some ways, it is almost like writing a person's "last words." You want to get it right!

I remember trying to write Johnnie's obituary. Overwhelmed by the need to get it to the newspaper "on time" (and when was the deadline, anyway?), I couldn't think straight. All of the things I knew so well — where Johnnie had gone to school, what clubs and organizations mattered the most to him, all the amazing things he had accomplished — were suddenly gone, seemingly deleted from my memory bank. I was operating on autopilot, thinking and speaking in a haze that made my already fragile emotional state even more tenuous. Fighting the rising panic in my chest, I drove to the office to consult with Sam. Surely, he could take charge of this project and rein in my runaway anxiety.

Unfortunately, Sam wasn't any better equipped than I was. How could we sum up, in just a few paragraphs, the life of a man we so loved and admired? What could we write that would be worthy of his legacy? And why, after two decades of living and working alongside this remarkable man, could I remember almost nothing other than his name?

Looking back, I know I was in what I have since dubbed "the bereavement fog," a totally normal (and, thank goodness, temporary) condition that strikes with little or no warning. Had you told me then that what I was experiencing was perfectly normal, it would have eased the panic, but it would not have done anything to get Johnnie's obituary written and published. The filing cabinet at H.D. Oliver is brimming with prewritten obits, but it wasn't until I didn't have one for Johnnie that I realized the incredible wisdom of all of those families who'd had the foresight to get the job done.

So here's my advice. When it comes to obituaries, consider writing your own. I know, I know — that can sound sort of creepy. But really, who could do it better? And who knows? This could be the best fifteen minutes of fame you ever get! (A word of caution, though: Take care not to embellish your accomplishments too much. Funerals are the one time most people will say only nice things about you; don't give anyone a reason to go off script.)

Don't see this as an intimidating project; if you aren't sure where to start, just open the newspaper and use what you find in the obit section as your template. And your funeral home can help. They will provide the fundamentals (things like where the service will be held, and when); all you need to do is — ahem — provide the body.

Here's an idea of what you might want to include:

- List your church membership, as well as your affiliation with any significant organizations or clubs.

- Note your occupation, and consider highlighting your interests or accomplishments.

- Write a sentence or two about your background, particularly if you were raised in another part of your state or country and want to provide a connection point for your friends and family members.

- Be sure to mention your surviving family members by name, and note where they live.

- Finally, list any favorite charities or organizations to which people can make memorial donations in your name. Many people prefer making a charitable contribution to sending flowers as a token of their love or sympathy.

Remember, too, that — tempting as it may be — an obituary is not the place to get in the last word. No railing against those who have hurt or offended you during your life, and no discussion of family feuds or secrets. And if you choose to include a photo, please be sure it is a fairly current one; you don't want your heirs to find themselves deluged with callers who care less about expressing their sympathy than they do about discovering the name of your plastic surgeon!

Writing your own obit will save your family a great deal of stress and anxiety at a time when any such relief will likely come as an overwhelmingly welcome gift. You might even consider doing it *with* your family. Distilling a life into a short newspaper column can highlight the things that matter, spark some interesting conversation, and provide a window into your life and accomplishments by shining the spotlight on milestones your family might otherwise miss.

Years ago, I asked my father to write his obituary. I love him dearly, but I was too young or too self-absorbed as a teenager to remember many of his accomplishments. My mother knew, of course, but when she passed away, she took a wealth of memories with her. Left to my own devices, I would be sure to omit something vital from my father's remarkably stellar life.

As would my own daughters, were they to write about me. They'd get my name right, I think, but they wouldn't know my birthday, since I haven't been exactly forthcoming about my age for the past couple of decades. Here's what I imagine their efforts might produce:

> VIRGINIA BEACH — Deona Chesley Branch Oliver, ?? [the girls would probably make up an age or just leave it out], passed away on _____ [they'd get the date right; the funeral home would make sure of that]. Born someplace in California, Dee graduated from Norfolk Catholic High School [here they would start cracking up and have to take a break; for some reason, my kids think it is hilarious that I went to a Catholic school], then went to college someplace, and then went back to school to get her degree in mortuary science. She was the daughter of Jacquie and Deon Branch.
>
> Dee was predeceased by her husband, Johnnie [the girls would forget to include their dad's full name], and is survived by her daughters, Jacquie, Madison, and Aven. She worked at the funeral home, and when she wasn't doing that, she could be found working out at the gym, playing tennis, or attending garden club meetings.

> She had a lot of cousins, and her dogs followed
> her everywhere she went. She talked on the
> phone — a lot! She loved God and her husband,
> and she always made her kids go to church.
> *[At this point, the girls would probably get bored
> and decide that my obit was complete.]*

If that's your idea of a good obituary, then by all means, leave it to your kids. But if you want to have any say in the matter — and certainly, if there's any chance they could use one of those photos you meant to delete from your files — then grab your pen and get started. And at the risk of sabotaging what could otherwise be a romantic evening, you might even consider scheduling a "date night" with your spouse when you can work on your obituaries together. Put the completed copy with your wills, or give it to your funeral home to save for you.

And then don't think about it again.

Go ahead and live your life to the fullest, secure in the knowledge that, when you wake up one morning in your heavenly mansion and open the paper and find your name listed among the "newcomers," it really will be a good day.

FLOWERS, FOOD, AND OTHER WAYS TO SHOW YOU CARE

*O*ne of the perks of working in the funeral business, at least for someone who likes flowers as much as I do, is that you get to see all sorts of floral arrangements. It wasn't long after I started working with Johnnie before I learned to recognize which arrangements came from which florist, which flowers carried the headiest fragrance, and which ones had the most staying power on the altar and afterward at the reception or in the cemetery. It was, if you discounted the ever-present sadness of death, a garden clubber's dream.

Working in the funeral business is also an epicurean's delight — at least if you don't mind somewhat limited and often predictable fare. Johnnie loved the tea sandwiches at Galilee Church, the cookies at Eastern Shore Chapel, the feta cheese and olives at Greek Orthodox receptions, and the literally to-die-for ham biscuits served up by the Princess Anne Country

Club. And he, like all seasoned funeral directors, could always tell you whether a reception would be dry (and the limo drivers could keep the car engines running) or whether it would feature an open bar (in which case the drivers would probably have time for a nap). In terms of knowing what to expect at each service, Johnnie and I considered ourselves to be pros. And when it came to knowing what people could do to show love and support, we thought we'd seen it all. Chicken salad? Check. Vase of flowers? Check, check. Warm and heartfelt condolence note? Check, check, check.

That was before Johnnie died. Being on the receiving end of a community's love opens your eyes to a whole new world of caring. No longer were the meals and flowers and notes that came into our house just evidence of a check mark on someone's to-do list; they became testimonies of thoughtfulness and love, of memories shared and treasured. They were markers of friendships that would endure through the grieving season, offering hope for the days that lay beyond the horizon.

Being on the receiving end, I learned there was a lot I didn't know. I learned, for instance, that even when an obituary reads, "In lieu of flowers, please make a donation to _____," you will still get flowers, particularly in the South, where people double up on condolences — making charitable gifts in a person's memory while still offering tangible support in the way of food, notes, and flowers.

And truly, you can't go wrong with flowers. Flowers are a way of letting a family know you are thinking about them, and that they are loved. But here's a hint: An arrangement that arrives weeks, or maybe even months, after the funeral can really brighten a family's day by letting them know they are not forgotten.

Gifts of food are another much-appreciated way to show you care. After Johnnie's death, the idea of going to the grocery store or trying to put a meal together for the girls seemed next to impossible. I thought I would be able to get my act together in a few days (I mean, how hard can it be to whip up some mac and cheese?), but that really wasn't the case. I thank God, even now, for the friends and family members who kept the food coming, dropping off meals — even takeout entrees from our favorite restaurants — for weeks after the funeral. And, as with flowers, delivering a meal a month or two later, when the "urgent" need seems to have passed, can be incredibly meaningful.

(And here's a little-known culinary tip you won't see on the Food Network: If you are going to bring someone a dinner that consists entirely of Cheerios, throw in a bottle of red wine. Trust me, it makes a very satisfactory meal.)

If the thought of writing a heartfelt sympathy note gives you writer's block — and if it does, you're not alone — consider picking up the phone for a good, old-fashioned call. All you have to say is, "I'm sorry. I just want you to know I'm thinking about you." And even though it might make my mother roll over, I have to say that even just sending a text message isn't a bad idea; as sterile and impersonal as it sounds, it is *always* nice to hear from people. Whatever you do — whether it's a note in perfect penmanship, a gourmet dinner (delivered in disposable containers, please), or the briefest text message — remember this: To you, the gesture might seem almost inconsequential, but to the bereaved, a timely and encouraging word or a tangible expression of kindness can make all the difference. If nothing else, it sends the message that they are not alone.

If one of your friends has lost a spouse or other close family member, consider going to their house and simply doing what needs to be done. Water the flowers; if needed, replant them. Clean out the refrigerator (this is especially helpful after a few days, when the leftovers will need sorting). Remember my friend Leslie, the one who organized my entire Tupperware cabinet? It's a mess again now, but I will never forget how nice it was to have it all properly sorted, at least for a little while. (It really was a stellar accomplishment. Johnnie would have wanted to make love right there in the kitchen, had he seen all those tidy stacks with matching lids!)

Truly, any little thing you do will help. Sometimes something as simple as offering to give someone a ride to church or to another function, or to meet a widow or widower at a party, can be huge in terms of warding off things like loneliness, depression, and self-pity. Men, pay particular attention to widows who may need a gentleman to take their coat or get them a drink. That's not flirting; it's simply being attentive.

Research shows it takes about five years after someone dies for the surviving spouse to feel like himself or herself again, and that the second year is the hardest. When I first heard that, I thought it sounded a little bit dramatic. Maybe other people needed all that time to pull themselves together, but not me.

Once again, I was wrong.

When Johnnie died, followed shortly thereafter by my mother's passing, I thought my toes had curled in on themselves. I could hardly move. And as the weeks went by, and then the months, it didn't seem like I was making much progress. Finally, we marked the one-year anniversary of Johnnie's death, and I breathed a sigh of relief. *At last*, I thought, *I can get back on my feet.*

Not so fast. That second year really was the worst — in large part, I suspect, because everyone (myself included) thought I'd already conquered all of the big milestones (Johnnie's birthday, Fathers' Day, Christmas, our wedding anniversary, etc.), and I'd made it "through." But then, just when I thought things might get better, Grief would jump me from behind. Again.

It's been nearly seven years since Johnnie died. Somewhere along the way, maybe around the five-year mark, I realized I was still standing upright and moving forward, and so — thankfully — were the girls. Nobody flunked out of school; nobody is on drugs (unless you count the occasional Tylenol PM); and nobody has run off and married the lead singer in a rock band (although, if I am to be honest, I must tell you there were plenty of days when I thought about it).

So thank you to all of my friends for the times you brought us a meal — and then stayed to eat it with us. Thank you for sitting with me at church, joining me on a walk, or inviting me to your dinner parties, even when you had to pull up an odd chair. Thank you for loving me, and thank you for loving my girls.

We will never forget it.

DOS AND DON'TS
FOR THE BEREAVED

When you lose a loved one, you'll find yourself on the receiving end of a lot of commentary. People will tell you what you should eat, where you should go, whom you should date (or not date). In a lot of cases, these people will be your friends (or they will consider themselves as such), and you might think it's rude to ignore their entreaties. But as long as I'm dishing up advice on everything from obituaries to flowers, I guess now's as good a time as any to throw out a few "do's and don'ts" of my own, targeted specifically to the recently bereaved.

The bad news is that you might not like my advice.

The good news is that you can feel free to ignore it.

A few months after Johnnie died, and after a particularly long, hard week filled with pity parties for myself, I went to the cemetery. Standing over my husband, I looked down on his grave and stomped my foot. "Tag!" I yelled. "You're it!"

What I meant — and what I am sure Johnnie would have

understood, had he been listening to me instead of hanging out with his buddies in heaven, swapping grilling tips and eye-balling the celestial lawn for any sign of weeds — was that I needed a break. I was tired of being a single parent. A single bill payer. A single party guest. I was ready for Johnnie to get up and take his turn.

Here's the thing. It's not going to be easy. You will get tired. You are bound to make some mistakes. You might think you'd know what to do when you lose a spouse — I certainly thought I could figure it out, having been part of a family that had more than 160 collective years of helping people through the adjustment process — but, like most people, I had to learn a few lessons the hard way. And so, for what it's worth, here's my take on survival:

Don't drink an entire bottle of red wine, consume a large bag of potato chips with onion dip, and watch an episode of *Law and Order*. You never really enjoy wine in large quanti-ties; potato chips and onion dip don't actually count as a serv-ing of vegetables, and the TV show is depressing. If you make the same mistake I did, all you will have to show for your evening is a headache, a bad mood, and a pair of pants that won't button.

Do get up and out of bed every day. And then make it. You will be far less likely to crawl back under the covers if your bed is made.

Do take a shower. I realize this may sound obvious, but sometimes it's the little things that can be the hardest. (And you may even learn something: I didn't know until I tried it that it was actually possible to wash your hair, shave your legs, cry your eyes out, and throw up all at the same time.)

Don't cut your hair, or dye it red or blonde or your natural gray, or get indigo blue highlights, no matter how hip you think they might make you look. Remember the "no change for a year" rule? Indigo highlights, along with things like nose piercings and tattoos, are one of the reasons this rule was invented.

Likewise, if you are a man, *don't* grow a beard or a mustache. (Ladies, if you notice signs of a mustache on your upper lip, feel free to go ahead and get that waxed. The tenets of basic hygiene trump the no-change rule.)

Do take vitamins and get Botox. Both will make you feel good!

Don't rely on sleeping aids, at least after the first couple of weeks. Sleeping alone after years of marriage can be strange and unsettling; the bed seems to be twice the size it used to be, and every noise and creak you hear may have you poised to dial 911. (One night I was certain a burglar was downstairs. I couldn't find my reading glasses or the phone, so I started punching random numbers into the alarm pad, hoping to set it off. By the time I fell over the ottoman, yelled at the dogs to wake up, and found the phone, I realized the noise was just that — a noise. Eventually, I learned how to sleep by myself, and I now sleep almost as soundly as the dogs.)

Do exercise. Not only will it help physically; it will also provide a good emotional outlet for all of the adrenaline that seems to be coursing through your veins at 100 miles per hour.

Don't buy a new pet. (Again, see the no-change rule.)

Don't take up smoking.

Don't shop online late at night when you feel alone and pitiful. Trust me. Late-night shopping only adds worry to an already sleepless night once you realize you didn't really need whatever it is you bought, you shouldn't have spent the money, and you are now going to have to go to the post office to send it back.

Don't cry in public — or at least try not to. It only makes the people around you feel awkward, since they won't have any idea why you have become unglued.

Do, however, identify a couple of friends with whom you can fall apart. Be sure to let these people see you when you are happy too — but don't be afraid to be vulnerable with people who truly love you.

Don't yell at your kids when they haven't done anything wrong. When you forget this rule (which you will, and which I did — more times than I care to admit), *do* apologize, and quickly.

Do invite people over for dinner, even if you order takeout food.

Don't worry about saving the environment; feel free to use paper plates. (Johnnie did our dishes every night. He took what I'd always considered a "pink" job and made it thoroughly "blue" as he commandeered the kitchen sink after dinner. The first night I cooked for the girls after Johnnie died, we all got up from the table and walked out of the room. An hour later, Madison and I walked back into the kitchen and — lo and behold! — it was still dirty. We looked at each other and made a quick decision: for the next few weeks, our china pattern would be anything made by Chinet or Dixie.)

Do tackle your paperwork. Take your time.

Do date. No, wait —

Don't date.

I don't know. But I do know this: Ladies, *don't* marry the first guy who asks, if you are still mourning the loss of your husband. And men, *don't* ask the first woman who brings you a casserole to marry you, even if you can't figure out how to turn on the oven by yourself or run the washing machine. Get some takeout food and hire a housekeeper until you have had time to heal.

And *do* go out. Attend meetings, luncheons, and parties. You don't have to stay long; eventually, you will want to. After Johnnie died, I took myself out to dinner once a week. I'd go to a nearby restaurant, sit at the bar (which is less awkward when you are sitting alone than if you are at a table), and have dinner. Nine times out of ten, I would see someone I knew, chat for a bit, and then go home. I can't begin to explain how hard this was to do at first, but I knew I had to relearn how to go out. Pick a place where you feel comfortable — a familiar spot, close to your home — and get dressed. You can't stay home forever.

Do smile. Pretend to be fine. With practice, you will start to believe it, and with time, it will start to be true.

Do start your day well. Every morning, I begin with a cup of coffee and God. I pray through my fears (large and small) and talk to God about my hopes and dreams. Sometimes I have a good cry — but with God, even the tears serve a purpose. It's nice to know he understands, and that he has the power to help me.

Do end your day well too. My evening routine is pretty much the same as the morning, except instead of coffee, God and I often enjoy a glass of good red wine. I thank him for my girls and for all the ways he has cared for us and provided for our needs. I thank him for bringing me through another day, in spite of all my frailties. I thank him for the unexpected setbacks that may have surprised me and for the confidence I have that he will work these things out in good time.

I especially thank him for giving me the blessing of family and friends.

And then, with a heart so full of gratitude that there isn't much room left for sorrow to find a place to camp, I go to sleep.

PICK A TEAM

or Christians, this present life is the closest they will come to Hell," writes Randy Alcorn, the author of a book called *Heaven*. "For unbelievers," he says, "it is the closest they will come to Heaven."*

Johnnie got that. Always fairly private about his personal beliefs, he didn't use words like *believer* or *unbeliever*. Instead, he usually put it like this: "You have got to pick a team."

He was speaking, of course, about a religious team. Perhaps you are already on one. Maybe you are even a "starter," playing every Sunday and actively participating in things like Bible studies or Sunday school. Lord knows, there are plenty of good teams out there: big teams and little ones, traditional teams and more contemporary versions, quiet teams and those with loud singing and shouting and hands in the air. Baptist, Lutheran, Catholic, Episcopalian, Presbyterian, non-denominational — you name it, and you can probably find it.

And here's the thing about being on God's team. It doesn't

---

* Randy Alcorn, *Heaven* (Carol Stream, IL: Tyndale House, 2004), 28.

matter how talented you are or whether or not you are in shape. You don't even have to know the rules of the game to join. And there are no cuts. You just ask for a spot, and you're in!

It helps, though, to show up for practice. You want to know where the locker room is, and when the coach comes out in his white clergy robes (or his suit, or even his blue jeans, as is the case with some franchises), it's nice to know he recognizes you. Oh, and if you joined the team as a youngster and your parents filled out your forms, you might want to check the roster to be sure your name is still there. Every player has to sign up for himself or herself.

In terms of end-of-life planning, being on a team has at least two distinct benefits.

The first is that it makes everything easier for your family. A funeral home can arrange for a religious official to conduct your service if you don't have a team, but it's much more comfortable if the guy who's giving the play-by-play of your life knows a little bit about you and your family. Not only that, but when the funeral is over and everyone goes out for a bite to eat and life begins to move forward again, you'll want to know that your loved ones are surrounded by "teammates" who care, people who will be with them to offer love and support, inning after inning, quarter after quarter, lap after lap.

(I say this both as a professional and from my personal experience. When Johnnie and my mother passed away within four months of one another, I am not sure I could have returned to the playing field were it not for the "coaches" and my "teammates" at Galilee Church.)

The second benefit is, of course, for you. Borrowing a bit here from Randy Alcorn, you've got to ask yourself whether you want this present life to be the closest you ever get to heaven ... or to the other place.

I can't tell you how many funerals I've been to where the minister says something like, "Tom was sick, and he knew he didn't have long to live. He came into my office one day, wanting to be sure he'd wind up in heaven." It's a fair question.

Not long ago, I attended a funeral for a prominent philanthropist, a man who'd probably done more good for our community than anyone. During the service, the minister recounted the time he and the man had spent together, reflecting on the fellow's legacy of service in everything from education to business development to caring for the poor and needy. The philanthropist hoped, the minister said with a smile, to get a little bit of "credit" for his good works.

And he did. Everyone—both on this side of heaven and on the other side—knew how generous the man had been and how many lives he had impacted and improved. "But," the minister said, "we also talked about how salvation doesn't depend on man's good works but on the good work that Jesus has done on our behalf." The philanthropist agreed with that assessment, and when he asked for a Bible verse that would sum up their conversation, the minister shared the simple truth of Romans 10:9: "If you declare with your mouth, 'Jesus is Lord,' and believe in your heart that God raised him from the dead, you will be saved."

Johnnie was no preacher, and he couldn't have quoted

Romans if his life depended on it, but he definitely understood the need to "declare with your mouth" and "believe in your heart," particularly since most people have no idea when they might actually need that assurance of salvation. "We mark our birthdays on the calendar every single year," Johnnie used to say. "Our death day goes by every year too—we just don't recognize it."

Never one to push his faith on anyone, Johnnie was nonetheless adept at raising the subject, if only to ascertain what sort of service a person might wish to have. One day, a well-known and very successful businessman walked into his office. The man had come to make his funeral arrangements. As the two of them discussed the various aspects of the service, Johnnie asked about his religious affiliation.

"None," the man answered. He didn't believe in God or the afterlife. "Once you're gone, you're gone," he said.

"Are you sure you don't want to pick a team?" Johnnie asked gently. After all, if the fellow was right and God didn't exist, he hadn't lost anything. But if he was wrong—if there was, in fact, an eternity waiting to happen—the man's gamble would have cost everything.

The man declined.

Later that night, as Johnnie and I discussed the day's events, his face grew somber. "You know," he said, "it takes a brave man or a fool to sit across the table from me, planning his own funeral, and not be on a team."

TRIAL RUN

You know that part in the wedding vows where it says, "In sickness and in health ... until death do us part"?

Well, there have been plenty of times since Johnnie died that I have asked God if I could please have my own first-class ticket to heaven, both to be reunited with Johnnie and other friends and family members, and — more pointedly — to have a change of scenery. Life on this earth can be, as we all know, a challenge at times.

For whatever reason, God has not yet chosen to honor my request. I can only assume he wants me to work on things like my fortitude and my character, and maybe even to replace the gutters on our house. I don't know.

All I know is that my to-do list seems to get longer every day. Paint the house. Replace the windows. Fix the air-conditioning and heating units. Fertilize the yard. Fix the car. Fix it again after one of the girls has an accident. Research college options. Figure out how to pay for college. Move my daughters into college. Learn how to be sick.

Learn how to be sick? Yes. That was apparently on my list — whether I knew it or not. I have long known how to take care of *other* people who are sick or otherwise infirm — my kids have all had the usual childhood injuries, colds, and flu, and my father is now in a wheelchair — but I guess God thought I needed to walk that road and learn how to trust him for myself too.

And I am not talking about your run-of-the-mill stomach virus, root canal, or even foot surgery, all of which are pretty much par for the course at our house.

I am talking about knock-down, flat-out, ER-hopping (I found myself in and out of our local hospital several times in a bizarre journey that ultimately landed me at Johns Hopkins), "this could be fatal" sickness.

I prayed I would survive, and I was fairly certain I would, but on the outside chance that I finally got my ticket, I wondered if I was ready. *Do I have everything in place? Can my children survive without me — without any parent?*

The answer, I am happy to report, is yes.

And if you set aside the fact that my kids had to endure an emotional roller coaster for several weeks, wondering when (or even if) I would get better, I would have to say that my "trial run" at the whole death thing was a success.

My medical directives and health insurance worked perfectly, and the people I asked to make medical choices for me passed their test with flying colors, comforting the girls and letting them know everything was under control. My will is complete and up-to-date. I have a good life insurance policy that will take care of the children's material needs, and my funeral has (finally) all been arranged. My legal advisers and trusted friends know where I keep my important papers, which banks I do business with, and what sort of dreams and plans I have for my children. Everything in my life, it seems, has been signed, sealed, and notarized!

Noah didn't get to take the ark on a trial run; the rain just started coming one day. Thankfully, he had done all the prep work—and he was ready! I hope you never have to go through a trial run either, but if you do (and even if you don't!), I hope you float.

FILLING THE HOLE

*B*efore I became a widow, I would have told you that widowhood involves loneliness. I would have said it comes with a measure of sadness and heartache. I probably would have identified fear and uncertainty as two more unwanted guests at the table. What I wouldn't have predicted, as I cataloged these anticipated thoughts and emotions, is the incredible hollowness I felt. Johnnie's death left a void, to be sure, but the vacancy went beyond just the space he once occupied in my life. I felt ... empty.

I've had quite a while — more than seven years, actually — to adjust to my new role, and I've realized one thing about emptiness: It can't be filled from the outside; it has to be filled from within.

Many people have looked at my life as a widow and asked me, "How do you do it? How do you get along so easily? How do you take it all — the grief, the loneliness, the going to church and parties and parent-teacher conferences all by yourself — in stride?"

And then, without waiting for me to reply, they think they

have it figured out: "It is because you and your husband were in the funeral business, right? You must just be used to death."

Um, no. You never get "used to" death. And if you were to ask me today how I have "done it," I would tell you this:

I have fallen down on this road countless times, so much so that I have the scars on my knees and hands to prove it.

I feel like I have shed enough tears to fill a swimming pool. I have lost my cool, blown up, yelled, screamed, stomped my feet, thrown up, thrown things, and wailed so loudly that I expected the neighbors to come running or call 911.

I have let myself down on many occasions. I have let my girls down even more.

I have woken up some mornings and groaned at God, angry at him for giving me another day.

I have not, in short, "taken it all in stride."

But I have done at least one thing right: I have prayed. And if I had to identify just one thing that kept me, kept us, on course and moving forward amid the chaos and uncertainty, I would point to that: prayer.

Yes, I said prayer.

I am not great at it. You'd think all those years with the nuns would have taught me something, but as far as praying goes, I am still a rank amateur. I am far from eloquent, and I've always been glad God doesn't mark down for things like bad grammar, incomplete sentences, or veering off topic. And I am no Bible scholar; I misquote the Good Book constantly, and I can almost never find a particular verse when I want it.

But every morning after Johnnie died, I would show up

with my coffee and my Bible and talk to God. Some mornings, I would do all the talking; others, I'd mostly just try to listen. There were plenty of mornings when our conversation consisted mostly of me just crying. I'd cry a little, say his name, and then cry some more.

But I always showed up, and he was always waiting for me.

He was waiting, I realized after a while, to help me fill the large empty hole. Slowly, and gently, he did.

Looking back (and you know hindsight is 20/20), it was a journey I wouldn't have traded. I know it sounds crazy. After all, over the last seven years I have lost my dog, my husband, and my mother. I got so sick I nearly died myself, and then I found out I could no longer work at my husband's company. Somewhere in there, I began to think my middle name must be Job.

But if God had come down, even at my lowest point, and said, "Dee, would you like me to put it all back for you the way it was?" I would honestly have said (and I would still say), "Thank you, but no. I think we are good."

I say that because of the way the girls and I have healed. Oh, we are not through; God definitely has some more work to do. But as I look at how he has taken care of us, I can't help but notice the character he has developed, particularly in my daughters. My girls have a strength and fortitude that wasn't there before, and they are filled with qualities like grace and mercy. They have been gifted with an understanding that, I think, extends beyond their years: They know what's important, what really matters.

None of that would have happened if our lives hadn't taken the jagged and broken turns that came with Johnnie's death.

As for me, well, I have always understood that life is a gift. After all, I am a funeral director. But through this journey — unwelcome though it was — my faith has become stronger, and I have learned to trust God as both my Lord and my friend. He has filled my heart with love. The hole is closing, and I am blessed.

So what's the secret to surviving the loss of a spouse? I don't really know, at least not in a neat and tidy way. But I know the best place to begin.

With prayer.

The Lord is close to the brokenhearted ...

PSALM 34:18

EPILOGUE

I was going down the road not long ago, riding shotgun with a good friend behind the wheel, when we happened to pass a cemetery.

"Lift up your feet!" my friend shouted.

"What?"

"Your feet!" he repeated. "Get 'em up off the floor!"

"Why?" I asked as I picked my feet off the floorboards. "Why am I doing this?"

"Because that's what you do when you pass by a cemetery."

"Really?" I had never heard that one. "Why?"

"I don't know," my friend admitted. "It's just what you're supposed to do."

I burst out laughing. Here I thought I knew everything there was to know about headstones and burial plots — my favorite cemetery being the Hollywood Cemetery in Richmond, with its rolling hills, mature trees, and quiet beauty (a side effect of the occupants being, of course, mostly silent) — but I had never heard of the "feet up" rule.

I guess you never stop learning.

I know I still am. Maybe not about cemeteries (although

217

goodness knows, there is *plenty* to discover on that subject, even for someone who spent some of her best years pushing baby strollers between headstones, using grave markers to help her children master their ABCs, and then agonizing over the *location, location, location* question when it came time to find a new home for her beloved), but about life. And about making plans. And about trusting God when nothing you planned for, or expected, turns out the way you thought it would.

I thought the biggest test of my trust would come in the weeks and months after Johnnie died, as I learned to depend on God for everything from our material needs to our emotional health. And in some ways, that was the biggie. What I didn't reckon on, though, was having to learn how to do the trust thing all over again at virtually every turn. When it first hit me that I was going to have to raise three active girls (with no one to slip them Pepsi and hot dogs behind my back). When I found myself back in a college chemistry class (and in way over my head). When I tried to get a job in my husband's company (and felt the door slam in my face). And when I needed to finish a three-thousand-hour internship (and wound up working among people with whom I had absolutely nothing, and absolutely everything, in common).

Now I am in a new place of trust.

I have my graduate degree; I have my internship hours; and I have my official funeral director's license, signed, sealed, and delivered by the great state of Virginia. The only thing I don't have yet is, ahem, a job. It's like I am all dressed up, and, well, you know ...

But if I've learned one thing about God, it's that (and I know I will probably misquote this verse too, but I am pretty sure it's from Isaiah 55) my plans are not his plans, and my ways are not his ways. His thoughts, the Bible says, are "higher" (which I can only assume means "better") than mine.

Which is a mighty good thing. Because right now, I am not even sure I have any plans, unless you count garden club or my workout schedule (and even that falls apart sometimes). I got appointed to a post on the Virginia Beach Planning Commission (because evidently, knowing how to plan your own life is not a prerequisite to mapping out a strategy for an entire city). And I wrote this book.

So I guess that's something. But I haven't shaken my desire to work in the funeral business, both as a way to honor Johnnie's memory and because I think I am actually good at it, and I want to be able to help people. I have no idea when — or even if— God will make that vision a reality, but I've given up trying to figure him out. Instead, I'll just camp out where I have learned to be comfortable — in a place of trust.

But that doesn't mean you won't catch me eyeballing any cemeteries I happen to pass. I can't help it. Crazy as it sounds, those places always make me think of Johnnie. I drove by one just the other day, and I smiled.

(I did not, however, lift up my feet.)

ACKNOWLEDGMENTS

I had the best time writing this book! And I couldn't have done it without about a zillion other people, including my good friend and God-given cowriter, Jodie Berndt. We worked out all the stories — literally — on the elliptical machines at the Princess Anne gym, where they have a "no cell phone" policy but no official rules about laughing too long or too loud. To all of our fellow gym members: Please accept our apologies. And I hope, since I guess you are reading this book, that you can laugh too (and find it in your hearts to forgive us for interrupting your concentration).

Thanks, too, to the "Write On" team of girls — Lisa Robertson, Trish Ryan, Elizabeth Williams, and Mary Elizabeth Stone — who first encouraged me to put my stories on paper, and to Shep Jordan for taking my collection of blogs and making them into the book, *Going Out in Style,* which served as a launching pad for this one.

And to Sandy Vander Zicht, Londa Alderink, Dirk Buursma, and all the talented people at Zondervan — I know how rare it is for a publisher to accept an untested author, particularly one who talks a whole lot better than she writes.

Thank you for believing Jodie when she told you we'd be a good team and for polishing our work in the wonderful way that you did, from catching our mistakes and suggesting improvements to producing the perfect cover design.

To ALL my cousins, especially Vicki Dickerson Trexler (who insisted I go out with Johnnie even when I said no) — thank you for making family so much fun. Even if I live to be 111 (like our grandmother), I will never forget the kindnesses you showered on the girls and me in the weeks, months, and even years after Johnnie left us. Likewise, we never could have survived without the lifeline of love that came from so many faithful friends, including Denice Rudolph, Joan and Tom Lyons, Andrea Kilmer, Nadia and Martin Carney, Sandy and Eddie Garcia, Ann and Frank Malbon, Bo Mills, Barbara and Tom Joynt, Corrine Barbato, Barb Sessoms, Bev and Will Sessoms, Nene Doughterty, Nancy Cole, Amy Drescher, Beth and Dennis Manning and the faculty at Norfolk Academy, Paul Riddick, and the folks at Galilee Church, especially our wise and wonderful ministers, Coleman Tyler and Andy Buchanan (whose time on the rowing machine was punctuated all too often by the Bible questions and sermon suggestions Jodie and I tossed over the elliptical — sorry about that).

And finally, to those I hold most dear — to my parents, Jacquie and Deon Branch, who loved me unconditionally (even when they had to hide out in Florida to escape the social fallout from my wedding plans) and taught me how to embrace and enjoy life, even in the most unimaginably painful and difficult circumstances; to my children, Jacquie,

Madison, and Aven, who are the most precious and wonderful gifts Johnnie and I could have ever asked for (and who are also the reason I need to color my hair and get Botox); and to God, who showed up every day, grabbed me by the hand, and pulled me into life so he could cover me with the blessing of his love — *thank you.*

(And God, if it's not too much trouble, would you mind telling Johnnie how much I love him? And ask him to please not be mad that I told about him going outside buck naked, with a shotgun, to get rid of the ducks in our pool. Thanks.)